Sh~~~

Thank you for
bring brilliant in
what you teach

♡ S~~~

UNDERNEATH IT ALL... YOU'RE NAKED

Shedding light on
misconceptions about sex
from a Christian wife
to Christian women

SARAH CHAPMAN

UNDERNEATH IT ALL... YOU'RE NAKED
Shedding light on misconceptions about sex from a Christian wife
to Christian women
Sarah Chapman

Published by Mental Work Publishing

Copyright © Sarah Chapman, 2020
ISBN 9798603101330

Publisher: Mental Work Publishing
                     220 N 1300 West, Suite 4
                     Pleasant Grove, UT 84062

Printed in the United States of America

CONTENTS

FOREWORD

By Trent Chapman, Sarah's Husband

We were hurt, frustrated, and contemplated ending our marriage. This was the state of our relationship after 12 years of not knowing how to communicate, not connecting sexually, and feeling misunderstood, unappreciated, and unwanted by each other.

I'll start with a little of our history so you can understand where Sarah has come from. This will illustrate how much has changed from what she has learned and implemented in her life. The things she shares in this book come from our experience and her choices to learn and grow.

We married in 2001, both virgins in our early 20s, and have been figuring out life together ever since.

As I started to explain, our marriage was not in a good place in 2013. Most marriages have rough patches and it is never fun. This rough time in our marriage was caused, in part, by our individual pride and in part because we didn't know how to communicate about the hard stuff. Because we didn't communicate well about the hard stuff, it became difficult to deal with everything else in our relationship. We both felt like running away.

That year I felt unwanted. I felt like Sarah didn't want to be with me and I felt I wasn't good enough. Our income dropped significantly and my new business was growing slow and demanded long hours. I tied my value to providing for the family and felt like I was less than the man she wanted or deserved. These doubts and fears grew more as we were not connecting emotionally, mentally, and physically as a couple. Our sex life was not great, and I always felt like it was a battle to get Sarah to talk about our intimacy and how we could improve and connect in that way. Years of feeling misunderstood caused me to seek out unhealthy ways to escape and cope. It added more burden to our already strained relationship.

Sarah had a lot of internal struggles around sex that I wasn't fully aware of, and what she did share with me, I couldn't comprehend why those things were hard for her. As a man, I thought, "we both saved ourselves before marriage, and now that we are married, how could you feel having sex with your husband is shameful or dirty?"

Because sex was such a struggle for her, I felt like she didn't love me or want to be with me. Most men are simple, but also we can come to strange conclusions. Allow me to illustrate. Most men feel appreciated and respected when their wife wants to have sex with them. Even more so if she initiates sex. Most men feel unappreciated and in a way disrespected when their wife doesn't want to have sex with them.

When I wanted to connect sexually with Sarah, but she wasn't in the mood, I took it as her saying, "I don't recognize your hard work to provide and I don't love you enough to allow you to connect with me through sex." The truth was, she didn't feel loved. I hadn't made her feel safe, and she had years of false beliefs and misconceptions about sex that made it feel like something "naughty".

From my perspective, it felt like I was not respected or appreciated for all the sacrifices and long hours I had put into working and providing so Sarah could be a stay-at-home mom. From her perspective, I was just focused on working and was gone 70 hours a week. She felt like she was on the path to being a single mom. When I wanted to connect physically with her, she just saw me as wanting to use her body for sex. It was not a healthy relationship, and we were both struggling.

We weren't taking time to connect. I wasn't serving her and dating her. We weren't sharing our fears, our dark sides, the things we struggled with, our dreams and our goals, or who we truly were behind the mask. I didn't share who I was out of fear. "If she really knew who I was and the temptations and struggles I face as a man, she wouldn't love me." My greatest fear was that if I let my guard down, Sarah would see all of me and not love me.

When we reached this low point in our marriage, Sarah made a choice to do something wonderful. She decided to work on herself. She started taking time to be more than just a "mom" and to take care of herself physically, emotionally, and mentally. Some might see that as selfish, but that is when I saw Sarah become a whole person. I love her for that. This not only changed her life, it helped change our marriage.

For years, Sarah has worked on how she sees herself and how she speaks to herself in her internal dialogue. She has worked on her physical health and strength by making time to work out. She has made time for personal study in all areas of her life to make her a more centered, well-balanced woman. Sarah shares this first part of her journey in her other book, *MindStrength for Women: How to go from feeling 'insecure', 'judged', and 'not good enough' to getting the body, relationships, and life you want and become "sexy confident"!* She truly went from being an insecure, perfectionist to this *sexy confident* woman that I always want to be with.

In 2017, after a few years of improving in all areas of her life, Sarah realized that sex was still something she needed to work on. She had made a lot of progress, but felt like there was still more. So she decided to start reading books about sex. She went to seminars and researched topics about human sexuality and the female anatomy. She truly worked on overcoming her limiting beliefs and learning more about the misconceptions she had held on to for years. This step took our relationship, connection, and marriage to another level.

Sarah was presented the opportunity to start teaching other women about their sexuality and sexual health in January 2018. She realized talking about sex, although taboo in Christian culture, was something that needed to be done. She has since taught, and worked one-on-one with hundreds of women.

This book is full of information gleaned from the dozens of books Sarah has read, the seminars and programs she has gone through, the hours and hours of conversations we've had together, as well as hundreds of conversations with women.

While Sarah isn't a licensed sex therapist, she has lived it, studied it, and helped other women go through the same journey of learning and growth. The concepts in this book are based on Sarah's studies, our real-life experiences, as well as the experiences of the women she has worked with. These concepts can be used to start conversations with your spouse and can have a major impact on your marriage and sexual relationship.

The more confident Sarah has become over the past seven years, the more we've been able to communicate and connect. This has inspired me to improve and work harder on myself. My desire to stay healthy and work out has increased. My ability to focus and provide for our family has increased. My desire for Sarah has increased. I want her more than ever, and I want to be the man she deserves.

The more we communicate, the more I trust her and let her in to see all of me, to know all of me. I know that she has created a safe space for me to share. She has been curious to know me instead of judging me for my weaknesses. This approach of curiosity has strengthened my trust in her and our marriage and allowed me to be curious as she shares all sides of herself with me.

This listening with curiosity has allowed Sarah to share all of who she is with me. We are able to explore more of what our fears are, more of what our goals and dreams are. We can share the little things we had been hiding from each other for most of our marriage. At first, this was scary for both of us, but communicating authentically and with full vulnerability allowed our relationship to grow.

Looking back, neither of us knew how great marriage could be. Now, I feel connected to Sarah like never before. I can share everything with her; the negative thoughts and doubts, the temptations and feelings of not being good enough. I don't feel like I have to pretend to be almost perfect for her to love me. We have created a relationship of trust, love, and connection. As we help each other grow and progress as individuals, we also grow and progress in our marriage relationship.

The reason I share some of our story is to say this. If you are in a marriage that isn't what you want it to be, or if you struggle with sex and physical connection, or if you just don't feel good enough, confident enough, whole enough, then please read what Sarah has to share. We've been in some pretty rough spots (this Foreword isn't our full story, but more is in the book), and Sarah has taken herself from being a woman I loved, but didn't know if I could be with, to truly my best friend and the person I most want to be with and be like.

Change can happen, and that change can affect all of those around you. It is scary to change, but when those changes are positive, life is bound to improve, and your relationships will too. The topics in this book should be used as conversation starters with your spouse. Read each chapter and think about how you can have a judgement-free conversation as you each listen to the other with curiosity and a desire to understand each other.

A NOTE FROM MY PARENTS

We acknowledge our lack of communication has caused challenges and misconceptions for you Sarah and your siblings and their spouses. Among our conservative Christian friends, we didn't have conversations about how we could prepare our children and their future spouses. Unfortunately, we followed the example of our parents and probably generations before them. We were told not to have premarital sexual relations. It is hard even now to write the words; it was such a taboo topic. There weren't any discussions about the mechanics of our body.

One cannot teach what one doesn't know or understand. And it seemed impossible for us to articulate what little we did know, even to each other. Thank you for teaching us.

It takes great courage to be so open about this very sensitive subject. Only a desire to help others in similar situations would prompt you and Trent to share such deeply personal stories. We are grateful that Trent is so supportive of you and your desire to teach others. You could not do it without his love and help.

Education is liberating. Freedom from shame. Realizing God created us to be as one. United as husband and wife. Married couples of our generation will also find the wisdom and suggestions of this book helpful to their marriage.

We are so happy you are breaking the cycle. As you have age appropriate, healthy sexual conversations with our grandchildren during their lives, they will learn the correct perceptions. It will not be a "dirty" subject. They will gain the knowledge they need to start their marriages right. We love you. Please forgive us. Go change the world one married couple at a time.

Love, Mom and Dad

INTRODUCTION

"UNDERNEATH IT ALL... YOU'RE NAKED"

One autumn day while I was sitting in my car, a video popped up on my Facebook newsfeed. The man in the video had a shirt with those words on it!

Those words caught my attention right away. I had been praying to find an answer to what I should title this book, and I couldn't get these words out of my mind for the next few days. I felt a stirring within me that that statement was to be the title of my book. But why those words? Then it came as clear as day.

As women, we tend to put on a shield to protect us and keep others away from getting deep into our minds and hearts. A shadow--you could say--that envelops our bodies. For most of us, it is a learned tactic to help keep us safe. We don't want others to really see our true naked selves.

Underneath our layers, if we choose to, we can find freedom and curiosity to explore who we really are and how we want our marriage to be.

This book's purpose is to shed some light on many misconceptions I had about sex and what my beliefs were surrounding it. I think you will find that you can relate to a lot of these, if not all of them.

mis·con·cep·tion / miskən'sepSH(ə)n/
noun

a view or opinion that is incorrect because it is based on faulty thinking, ignorance or misunderstandings.

You are responsible for what you've believed and who you have become as a result. But with this acceptance of your present beliefs and situation, you also gain control. If your old beliefs no longer serve you, you can choose to analyze, examine, and adjust your views and beliefs.

Misconceptions can get in our way of growth and connection. The goal of this book is to help you identify, analyze, and adjust your beliefs about sex so that you have a healthier, more empowered view about your body and sex.

Why is analyzing your beliefs about sex and examining them so important?

"Because it's impossible to go somewhere new, to become something new, without first acknowledging where you are."
    --Rachel Hollis, author of *Girl, Stop Apologizing*

Our society, the media, our families, and even our churches send us different messages about our sexuality. These messages have been playing over and over in our minds and have become so loud for so long that it's become white noise to us.

So I'm here to bring to your attention some of the things you may be struggling with at the core in your marriage.

That's why I do what I do. It's why I invest time in learning about the human body, our sex organs, and emotional connection. It's why I teach groups of women about sexual connection and how their bodies work. It's why I've read and researched different ways to look at what I chose to believe about sex. Ultimately, it boiled down to one thing:

I finally wanted to do sex well because I deserved it.

From there, I felt a deep desire and the need to help other women. I truly wanted to help women go from where I was in my marriage and my beliefs about sex to where I am now.

I've talked about it all: struggles in my marriage, contemplating divorce, pornography, feeling jealous, resentment, scared and just down right broken. I wanted to write this book to be totally real about who I am and where I'm coming from. I wanted to give hope to others who might also feel like they are broken or that something is "off" in their marriage.

My journey started with a series of "what if..." questions.

- What if I could replace the misconceptions that I've grown to believe into something different and positive?

- What if I enjoyed sex?

- What if I embraced my sexuality?

- What if I was able to express myself sexually?

- What if I became the spouse with more desire?

- What if God put this in my heart for a reason?

Then, a year into my journey, this last "what if..."

What if I could write a book that would help women view sex differently?

That "what if" was my potential knocking at my heart and begged me to find the courage to talk about this taboo topic with other women.

I've surprised not only those who have known me for over 30 years, but also myself. I never thought I'd be so open to talking about sex and sharing my struggles and the issues I've dealt with in my marriage. My questioning of old beliefs and asking myself these "what if" questions has led me to pursue something I never would have considered just a few years ago.

Are you wanting to pursue the answer to some of these "what if" questions for yourself?

I decided to put each misconception I had about sex and connection in marriage into its own chapter. In each chapter I share the stories or reasons why I believed it and then share things I learned or figured out that helped me adjust that belief or what changed my perception about it.

per·cep·tion / pər'sepSH(ə)n/
noun

1. the ability to see, hear, or become aware of something through the senses.
2. a way of regarding, understanding, or interpreting something; a mental impression.

It's not an overnight thing. It's a process to analyze, examine and adjust the basis of our beliefs that caused us to have these misconceptions. Be patient with yourself and your spouse as you go through this book. Be a student on this topic. I've strongly suggest you have a notepad, or take notes on your phone as questions are presented. Don't skip them thinking, "I'll come back to it later." I want you as the reader to actively write impressions on your mind as you go through it.

I didn't study sex extensively with the intent to become a sex or marriage and family therapist. I haven't studied psychology or human sexuality for decades like some experts. I found myself immersed in this subject because after being married for 16 years, I thirsted for it for the first time.

I wanted this book to come from someone you could relate with. I don't want to lose you in concepts and ideas that may be over your head. I've read a few articles and books where I left feeling more confused and lost because I couldn't understand the complex psychological concepts they were sharing, and I felt stupid because I didn't understand how it applied to me and my struggles.

I want to give you practical advice and simple solutions and things to work on now.

I don't have anything against therapists, but I've seen many marriages fail after thousands of dollars of therapy, where others have succeeded simply by both spouses learning how to be curious and try to understand their spouse without one or the other feeling pressured to attend counseling. It's not one person's opinion that will save your marriage. I saved my marriage on my own couch reading the thoughts from 30+ strangers on sex and intimacy in marriage.

Now before you think I am saying good sex is all you need to save a marriage, let me clarify. Sex isn't the thing that saved my marriage. Learning to talk openly about the most difficult subject for most couples (sex) has allowed us to learn to talk about, and listen to understand each other on finances, and how to parent and much more.

I remember the day where God put this in my heart to do this work. I ignored it for days and I remember feeling sick to my stomach that I was to talk about this topic that no one wants to talk about. I wrestled within my mind about the pros and cons to opening up after reading my library of books because I was ashamed that after 16 years of marriage I still hadn't figured out sex. But I have also learned that God rescues broken people. Your greatest contribution to this world will not be found in your natural strengths but in overcoming your weaknesses.

God uses ordinary people like me to recycle my pain for the benefit of others. I've noticed that when I share my pain and I'm honest about my weaknesses and misconceptions I had, I have been able to help others.

God allows pain to give us opportunities to minister to others. When we are hurting, we want someone who understands, someone who's been through what we've been through.

If you've struggled with sexual connection and communication about sex, I've been there too. I know your pain; I know how broken it can make you feel.

I want every woman to understand the nature of their sexuality and how God has designed their beautiful body.

Educating and empowering women has been a mission of mine the last two years, even before deciding to write this book.

Empowering means taking control of your life and choices and embracing the resulting freedom. When you're empowered, you know your worth; you are self-reliant and take responsibility for the choices you make. I share this sense of empowerment when I help other women face their fears and go after what they want. My goal is to inspire others to pursue their dreams and create a future that's better than they ever imagined.

In my first book I wrote in 2015, *MindStrength for Women*, I talk about helping women go from feeling "insecure", "judged", and "not good enough" to getting the body, relationships, and life they want and become "sexy confident."

However, in this book, I share with you my own inner journey on finding deeper meaning through sexuality. My goal in this is to help you develop the knowledge, confidence, and wisdom to make your sexuality a fulfilling part of your life, for the rest of your life.

I am dedicated to educating women to be able to make informed decisions about their sexuality by providing an opportunity to safely explore and understand their sexuality, gain confidence in their relationships with themselves and others, and help them gain insight into who they are as sexual beings created by a loving God!

> *"Sexuality is one of the foundations of a woman's sense of her own power, and when we truly learn to own, honor and respect this vital aspect of ourselves, we enrich every aspect and dimension of our lives. Yes, tips, bedroom accessories and techniques can lead us to great sexual pleasure, but that pleasure will not last unless it comes with an inner foundation of awareness and knowledge."*
> --Laura Brotherson, LMFT, CST, CFLE

I hear "thank you" from women not because they had a great night of intimacy with their spouse, but because they rediscovered themselves and found a new way to live their fullest potential.

My goal is to help women recognize the importance of sex in their marriage. I want them to gain confidence in conversations around their beliefs about sex that will lead to ultimately creating deep connection.

I believe in God and His Son, Jesus Christ, who is my Savior. I'm a Christian. I am a member of The Church of Jesus Christ of Latter-Day Saints and my perspective is as one who was raised in this church and as one raising my own children in this church. However, I have learned from my non-denominational bible study friends that many conservative Christian women also have grown up with and struggled in marriage with some of the exact same beliefs that I had. I will refer to us collectively as "Christians" throughout my book.

The three things I want you to walk away knowing from my book are:

1. Sex is for you.

2. Sexual shame disrupts love in all aspects. This shame eats at your emotions without you being aware of it.

3. Expressing your needs, desires, and wants about sex without judgment is critical for your marriage to thrive. So stay in a state of curiosity with your spouse.

DISCLAIMER

Extenuating circumstances may make some of these statements and ideas in this book untrue for you and your relationships, such as in cases of abuse. Abuse should never be tolerated and in cases where it is not extreme and where your spouse is working on changing, you will have to decide if the things I share in this book apply to your situation.

CHAPTER ONE

BELIEFS ABOUT SEX

"Do you know what's going to happen tomorrow night?"

It was the night before my wedding. My mother (who I love, adore, and respect) attempted for the first time to talk to me about sex. At 20 years old, I was young, but probably a bit old to be having "the talk" for the first time.

Of course, by this time I already knew what sex was; even though I had decided to remain a virgin, I'd already had "the talk" and learned things not on purpose from my friends in high school who were sexually active. My mother grew up the same way. Sex was not talked about in her home, so she didn't know how to talk about it with her children.

I replied to my mother's question with, "I think so. My friends have shared a few things, so I guess I'll figure it out."

My mom then went on to suggest I read a particular book on the topic written by a Christian author.

That was the end of "the talk," and the next night was not the greatest experience. I cried because of the pain I felt and felt super awkward in front of my new husband, Trent. I was also emotional because of the slight trauma this new experience had created because of the unknown. The following day I called my mother and cried some more. I wanted to express to her that I felt betrayed that she didn't tell me more. But I couldn't bring myself to hurt her and make her feel guilty that she didn't talk to me more. I felt even more confused about the mechanics of sex because we were left alone to figure it out.

From there, it took me another 12-15 years to learn what I wish I would have known before I got married, or at least during the first year or two. I could have avoided a lot of pain and frustration for both Trent and me had we learned how to communicate and change a few things, which we'll discuss in this book.

This isn't "the talk," as I won't be going into all the details of sex and anatomy in this book. I'll reference other resources I've found helpful. But this is for all you women out there, from 18 to 80, who never had a resource and never had the open communication around healthy sexuality as is the case in most conservative, Christian homes.

I want to focus on some very important ideas and concepts that will help you get the most from this book.

BELIEFS ABOUT SEX

God created us in his image. He is the master creator, the one who molded and shaped us to be, but our beliefs and negativity prove us otherwise. Could your beliefs be the problem?

> Do our experiences shape our beliefs?
>
> Or do our beliefs shape our experiences?

What great questions to ponder. We each may agree on one or the other, but I believe it can work both ways. Can we learn to manage our beliefs about sex in marriage? How difficult is it to maintain our beliefs?

Many women have been raised in families where sex was associated with judgment, shame, and other negative feelings. And while a woman may grow up thinking she has left these "outdated" views from home in the past, a negative belief system found in a conservative family or environment that looks down on sex can make a lasting and lingering impact on how women think and feel about sex, and ultimately themselves.

Growing up, I was taught at church and in my home that "sex is dirty." Maybe those weren't the exact words, but that's what I heard and began to believe. I'd heard comparisons to those who had sex before marriage as "chewed gum." "Nobody wants a piece of gum that has already been chewed!" What a sad thing to put into the mind of a young person who is already struggling with their self worth and finding themselves, especially for those who had been abused or experienced premarital sex.

While this belief that "sex is dirty" was false and sex in and of itself is not dirty or bad, that is the belief that I took from the few lessons I had about sex. Even though this belief was false at its core, it did serve me. It kept me from engaging in premarital sex, especially at an age when I would not be emotionally prepared to deal with those adult actions.

As a married woman, this same belief that once served me, that sex was bad or dirty, now caused some *major* problems. The belief that once protected me and served me in a way was now a hindrance to connecting with my husband! It took years before I finally challenged this belief, which eventually led me to challenge many other false beliefs about sex and intimacy. This allowed me to create a connected, fulfilling sex life and marriage that always seemed to be out of reach before.

As you read this book, please look at the beliefs that you hold on to and ask yourself, "does this belief still serve me in creating the connection I desire with my spouse?" If not, be courageous enough to challenge that belief and find out what is actually true. Remember, while a belief may have served us at one point, that is no reason to hold on to the belief forever.

If it is no longer serving us, but in fact blocking our progress in our relationship with our spouses, it's time to let it go and find out what is true.

Within your perpetual problems lie the greatest opportunity for growth and intimacy. I would consider my beliefs about sex a perpetual problem that turned into a solvable problem.

START THE CONVERSATION

This clearly isn't the Bible. It isn't the end all, be all to sex either. This book should help you to think differently about sex, but more importantly, it is a conversation starter. Use these topics to discuss sex in more detail with your spouse. The more you open up about sex with your spouse, the more you become one. Once it becomes easy to talk freely, without fear of judgment or criticism about sex, almost every other topic becomes easier! The goal is to grow so close that you feel as though you are one, to be so trusting and confident in your spouse that you know you can share anything with them and they'd never dare use it against you, belittle you, or make you feel like you are loved any less.

ASK QUESTIONS AND SEEK TO UNDERSTAND

Share things that you've been too afraid to share because of fear of judgment or criticism. However, before you can do that, you must first create a safe space in your relationship.

You are creating a safe space in order to have some extremely vulnerable conversations. Let's be real, sex is probably the hardest topic for most couples to freely talk about. Most couples don't share their most intimate thoughts, wants, or desires because they fear judgment. For many men, they are worried that, *"if my spouse knew this about me, they'd probably think I was weird and maybe want to leave me."* While you may laugh and think, "not me" or "not my spouse," I encourage you to hold back and not express that to your spouse, as you will only shut down your spouse from truly sharing. Even after 12 years of marriage, I learned so many things once I was ready to truly create a safe space to communicate with my husband.

I am not saying that vulnerable, raw, and open communication about sex is easy, or without consequence. I've shed many tears as I learned some things about Trent both that bothered me and that hurt because of the pain I had unintentionally caused him. I found out things that I had always assumed were not a part of other marriages. However, over the past few years I've come to find out that we are pretty normal, average, everyday Christians who struggled for years with sex. By opening up our communication with each other, we've been able to remove and overcome any unhealthy habits and create a new, stronger, more powerful marriage than what we had ever thought possible.

"Great Sarah, but my spouse won't talk about anything remotely vulnerable with me!"

Girl, I've been there and felt that. That's why we want to share with you a few things Trent and I have learned over the years to help us have vulnerable, real, raw conversations on a regular basis that allow us to grow closer and closer as we become *one*.

Please, read this following section at least twice and talk about it with your spouse *before* going on. In order to create a safe space to share, you need to set some rules that you both agree on.

YOU AGREE TO REMAIN CURIOUS AND NOT JUMP TO JUDGEMENT

If your spouse shares that they have had sexual thoughts about someone else, don't immediately assume they are a sick, cheating, no-good pile of garbage. That does nothing good for either of you.

Stay in a state of curiosity. Ask questions to clarify. Find out what has caused these thoughts or feelings. Sometimes, you'll find that there are things that you are doing that are unintentionally creating these unhealthy situations. Don't blame yourself, but also, don't judge or blame your spouse too quickly. Granted, there will be situations where wise judgment is needed; try to remain in a state of curiosity until making a judgement is necessary.

When we quickly jump to judgment, we shut down our minds from receiving more information and we shut down our ability to seek understanding for our spouse or feel empathy for them. That's an important point, so I want to repeat it. When we judge, we drastically reduce our ability to feel empathy for our spouse. We stop receiving information to better understand, and we instead look for things to further support our judgment.

> Try to remain in a state of curiosity and refrain from jumping to judgment.

If you have a long history of jumping down your spouse's throat about every little thing, this may take some time for your spouse to trust you enough to be truly vulnerable and share their deepest thoughts and feelings. We want the same reciprocity of refraining judgment when we share something vulnerable with our husbands, so we can do the same for them too. This isn't a quick fix or an overnight solution, but work at it and try to build back that trust and confidence so you can close the gap that may exist in your relationship. Vulnerable conversations only happen where there is a high level of trust. Trust that what you are sharing won't be met with harsh criticism, immediate judgment, or dismissal.

AGREE TO NOT BLAME EACH OTHER

This is a tough one. Just as it is easy to jump to judgment, it's also easy to want to blame. One reason why we encourage couples to not blame each other is that blame makes you powerless. Even blaming yourself doesn't do a lot of good. Acknowledging our contribution to a situation or problem and deciding how to improve next time is healthy. Dwelling on the past and using it as a weapon to hold onto hard feelings against yourself or your spouse isn't healthy. While your spouse may have legitimately done something that has hurt you and caused a bad situation for you, you can still choose to not focus on blame, but instead, focus on what *you* can do differently to change the situation or make it better going forward.

Yes, acknowledge the selfish or hurtful thing they've done, process the emotions and feel the hurt it has caused, but then choose what action *you* can take to change that so it doesn't happen again. You can't change how your spouse acts, but you can change your situation or how you act and react.

CHOOSE NOT TO BE A VICTIM

While a loving spouse will work on not repeating the situation, your spouse may or may not change. Don't hold on to blame to feel some sense of power. The power of accepting what you can change and then changing that is much more empowering than holding on to blame and hoping or waiting for someone else to change.

> Focus on being a creator, the one who seeks and finds solutions instead of remaining the powerless victim.

I believe God gave all of us the desire to create. He is the Great Creator and as His children, we have that desire to create. When we honor that desire and create and grow, we feel happiness and joy and fulfill our destiny as His children of infinite worth and potential. When we dishonor that God-given desire to grow and create, we feel unhappy, stuck and unfulfilled. Depression creeps in too.

Choose today to face and overcome the obstacles you've been avoiding.

Choose today to accept responsibility for all that you don't like about your life, your relationship, and your marriage. With accepting responsibility comes the power to actually *change* what you don't like.

Finally. Make a decision today that you are going to be a doer. Creators are doers. They don't look at problems and give up. No matter how many times things don't work out, they keep trying. They don't look at temporary set-backs as failure. They see them as one more way they have figured out that doesn't work and they keep *doing. You can do it.*

"In the growth mindset, you don't always need *confidence. When you think you're not good at something, you can still* plunge *into it wholeheartedly and stick to it. Actually, sometimes you plunge into something* because *you're not good at it. This is a wonderful feature of the growth mindset. You don't have to think you're already great at something to* want *to do it and to* enjoy *doing it."*

--Carol Dweck, author of *Mindset*

I'm living proof of this statement! I have plunged my heart and soul into my sexual health and connection with Trent, and now I'm here sharing it with you. I used to avoid sex. Be triggered by the thought of sex, and shut down and suppress every sexual part of my being.

I have questioned, cried, and threw my hands up many times, but I would always come back because I wanted to change and make my sex and marriage better. I now enjoy sex more than I ever thought possible.

Failure can be a painful experience. But it doesn't define me or you. It's a problem to be faced, dealt with, and learned from.

WHAT ARE YOUR BELIEFS ABOUT SEX?

Take a moment to really reflect and write down your beliefs about sex. Include both positive and negative beliefs. Make a list and have your spouse make a list and then start a conversation about what beliefs you have in common and try to understand the core of those that are different.

This is the starting point of understanding and analyzing beliefs that may need to adjust if they no longer serve you in your marriage.

CHAPTER TWO

SEX IS DIRTY, NASTY AND GROSS

I'll be the first person to admit it: I got married young. I was engaged July and married in September at the age of 20... way back in 2001. I had just completed my sophomore year at college. I was a virgin and so was Trent. We committed to keeping it that way until we were married.

Like many young Christian adults, I looked forward to my wedding and all the exciting changes it meant mentally, emotionally, and I was curious about the doors it unlocked with regards to physical intimacy. However, when I went to my physical exam, I quickly realized how vulnerable I had to be with a doctor and then realized that I had to expose myself to and be even more vulnerable with Trent.

Excitement about exploring this sexual intimacy that I'd heard my friends talk about at my bridal shower was turning to dread. This new experience of exposing all of me to my soon-to-be husband was frightening. I didn't know anything about my own body and how it worked, and I continued to leave it that way, even years after we were married.

I had no idea that I was signing up for a journey that would test my commitment to Trent and his to me as we struggled to figure out what movies and culture make look so easy: physical intimacy.

I bawled on my wedding night. And not the pretty "I'm so happy right now" kind of tears. On what was supposed to be one of the happiest days of my life, I was wracked by heart-wrenching sobs born of a deep sense of inadequacy and emotional pain. I couldn't make anything work. My mind was racing with questions; *how can I just jump into this?*

You might say I should have been expecting that. True, I had heard vague half-whispers that virgin newlyweds' wedding nights were nowhere near what the media would have you believe. What I didn't expect was that for many *years* I would place a mental block on sex. I didn't understand what intimacy was because I didn't want to be a "bad girl" (a label I placed on the type of girls who liked and were interested in sex).

I come from a Christian household where God was the center of our home. We believe that Jesus Christ is our Savior and the Son of God. I was taught at an early age to pray to God and we read from the scriptures. I came from a large family with 2 brothers and 5 sisters, plus two cousins who lived with use half of their childhood. You could say our house was busy, but as a child I never felt like I was neglected.

Sex wasn't an open topic at all in our home. Growing up in a religious home, all I would hear about sex was that I shouldn't do it. On the very rare occasions that sex was brought up, I was told, "no sex until you are married," but when I did get married, I sure had a hard time flipping the switch without feeling like I was naughty or unrighteous.

Outside of the home and amongst my friends I would hear about the bad girls having sex behind their parent's back and it made me believe that if I had sex, I would be dirty and a "bad girl." This is where my sexual shame started.

The definition of sexual shame that I found in Noel Clark's Ph.D. dissertation, The Etiology and Phenomenology of Sexual Shame: A Grounded Theory Study, states:

> Sexual shame is "a deep feeling of humiliation and disgust around one's sexuality, a belief of being abnormal, inferior or unworthy."

This shame developed as I interacted with family, my church culture, and the society around me. I felt like I was going in circles, getting the same messaging about fear and uncertainty in regards to my sexuality.

For years I wondered if I was alone in this. I wanted to be the "good girl" that honored God, but I couldn't figure out how to be the good girl and enjoy sex because of these beliefs and the misunderstandings I had around sex.

Women who were raised in an environment where sex was taboo or treated as shameful often have a hard time letting go of those negative feelings. One friend shared that in her house, her vulva/vagina were referred to as her "shame shame!" This may sound obvious, but I can't tell you how many women, including myself, not long ago, treat their sexuality as a negative thing, hiding from it themselves and keeping it hidden from their spouse. They are blocked from truly embracing their sexuality and the pleasure, connection, and love that it can bring to their marriage because they judge it as something bad, dirty, or morally wrong.

Most Christian theology emphasizes the importance of human bodies, so any discussion of marital love must begin with the premise that men and women are sexual beings and that sex within marriage is good.

Unfortunately, too many talks or sermons continue to focus on the temptations and harms of unbridled sexuality and what not to do, especially before marriage. Most Christian couples get very little instruction about what good and healthy sex is and what that might mean in a marriage, while being told many things that are bad and wrong about sex.

I would hear in church how God ordained sex as a sacred way to connect and create life between a man and a woman, but that's all I seemed to hear. It was one of those hush hush topics. Luckily (or unfortunately) I had a few friends who exposed me to some information about sex before I got married; otherwise I think I would have been completely naive as to the mechanics of sex.

Now I don't mean for it to sound like my parents completely ignored my education; it's simply that they didn't talk about sex openly. They chose not to expose us to the topic with the hope that not talking about it would mean we would abstain until marriage and hoping we'd just figure it out when we were old enough. I believe it was taboo to talk about sex in the conservative Christian culture where I was raised, which made it harder for my parents than it is for parents today. Plus, their parents didn't talk to them about sex, so they were just doing the best they could with what they knew.

As a child and adolescent, I believed everything that I was taught by my parents, church, and society about why sex before marriage was not a good thing. Although looking back, the way I was told to avoid sex before marriage created many of the negative beliefs I had around sex.

Some of the ways that adults tried to promote abstinence before marriage were not well thought out. While I am sure their intentions were good, the results have been devastating. A terrible example my husband experienced in a group class was just as horrifying as the chewed up piece of gum story I shared in Chapter One.

In his case, during a church lesson on sexual purity and abstinence a slice of bread was taken out of a bag. The instructor asked each of the 6 or so young men to handle the bread and look at it from all sides and then pass it along to the person next to them.

Once the bread had made its way back to the instructor, the question was posed, "now who wants to eat this bread that has been touched by everyone in this room?" Of course nobody wanted the bread, and they were then all offered a fresh, untouched slice of bread, which they each accepted. The instructor compared the first piece of bread that was passed around to someone who has sex with other people before marriage. The message was that nobody wants them!

Please! Let's stop these horrific metaphors and object lessons while attempting to teach abstinence!

Don't ever tell a young mind that they are not loved, not wanted, chewed gum, or a handled slice of bread if they have sex before marriage! This is not how God sees us. Of course we need to teach young people the sacred, powerful, and blessed connection that comes from sex and explain *that* is why they want to wait to have sex. We should teach them that they should wait until they are ready to connect in that way and are prepared for the consequence that is always likely--procreation of a child. Don't lead them to believe that they are not good enough or that they are going to hell if they make some decisions at a young age that may not be correct.

With your own family, or young minds you might have stewardship over, focus on the beauty of sex in marriage and the joy and pleasure that is found in a loving, committed relationship. To teach the benefits of abstinence, focus on the joy that comes from saving the power to procreate for a committed, loving relationship where children would be welcomed. When we shift from fear to focus on the positives, there is more hope that those who make mistakes don't give up on themselves or think they have lost value in God's eyes.

In spite of the good intentions of the teachers, we have been shown over and over again that lessons with fear based metaphors caused most of the listeners to have feelings of fear and anxiety and to receive other unintended negative messages about sexuality. This is unfortunate, because the Lord has taught that "if ye are prepared, ye shall not fear."

One of the primary consequences of fear-based object lessons and metaphors about sexuality is a negative portrayal of sexual intimacy, often unintentionally teaching to young minds that sex is a bad thing that harms us.

It is quite clear that many parents and teachers like to use object lessons because it has allowed them to talk about sex—without talking about sex. Please don't do object lessons when teaching young people about sex! Plus it shows you are uncomfortable with directly addressing the topic of sexuality.

These lessons are usually based on shame. When shame is part of the strategy to teach abstinence, it may work to some degree and cause some to avoid sex until marriage, but the shame and fear usually do not go away after marriage, as was my experience and that of countless women who I have worked with.

These metaphors also tend to discourage an open dialogue between young people and their parents about sexuality. Often in this context, young people feel that if they ask their parents questions about sex or show any interest in the topic, they could be labeled as "bad", "naughty", or "dirty." When they are curious, young people will seek out information where they feel safe from shame and judgment. When that doesn't exist with their parents or in their home they gravitate to friends, the media, or other outside sources to learn about sex—sources that are often not in harmony with Christian values.

It's important not to continue the habits of our parents, church and or society and instead to remove the shame from sex education as part of reforming your own sexual journey.

So when the day of our wedding arrived, our sexually inexperienced selves were supposed to throw off all our inhibitions, forget all the shame we'd been taught around sex and enjoy a full-throttled sex life right after the ceremony!

It doesn't happen like that. If it does, it's rare.

I had no idea of what to expect that night, and not understanding how to connect sexually made for a very long, exhausting night, which would continue into many more long, exhausting nights thereafter.

THE GOOD GIRL SYNDROME

I continued to accept sex as naughty, and although I enjoyed it for a moment once we were in the act and would allow myself to orgasm, I would immediately have guilt after we were done! I thought of it that way each time we had sex for *years*.

A lot of women are comfortable with giving pleasure but *not* receiving it. I felt like it was okay for Trent to want sex, to have sex with me, and to orgasm, but for some reason, I always felt like a bad girl if I allowed myself to feel those same things.

As the years went on, I wondered about the appropriateness of sexual relations within my own marriage. I convinced myself it was okay when we were trying to get pregnant, because that is the purpose of sex, right? Well, that's what I used to think. I believed that any "extra" sex for pleasure was dirty.

Can you relate with some of these thoughts that I struggled with?

If so, you may have heard of something called "The Good Girl Syndrome." This syndrome refers to the deeply internalized feelings and attitudes that emphasize negative associations with sexuality.

"The Good Girl Syndrome is a result of the negative conditioning that occurs from either parents, church, and/or society as they attempt to teach the importance of abstinence prior to marriage, but often fail to teach the goodness of sexuality and it's divine purposes within marriage. This then leads to negative thoughts and feelings about sex and the body, resulting in an inhibited sexual response within marriage."
--Laura Brotherson, LMFT, CST, CFLE

I originally heard about this concept from a book called, *And They Were Not Ashamed.*

As I prepared for marriage back in 2001 I tried to do everything right and kept myself morally clean. As a good girl, I assumed that since I had done everything "right," God would bless me and my marriage, and life would be great.

Here is a short list of symptoms of the "Good Girl Syndrome" that I found within myself. I've only shared a few, and I'm sure you can come up with some on your own that you've experienced. But I've provided it here to help you pinpoint and be aware of the negative conditioning you have unconsciously internalized and accepted:

- Discomfort, embarrassment or inability to appropriately discuss sexual matters

- Belief that sex is bad, wrong, dirty or sinful

- Inability to relax and let go within sexual experiences in marriage

- Inappropriate inhibitions, guilt, shame, or awkwardness associated with your sexual relations within marriage

- Discomfort and distaste with sexual parts of the body and bodily functions

I noticed I distanced myself from anything that would be perceived as bad. I didn't want to learn about taboo subjects because I knew Trent would try to ask me questions that I didn't want to answer.

I've had this internal question that I asked myself over and over for the first 16 years of my marriage:

"Why do I believe that sex is linked to being dirty, nasty and gross?"

But I really didn't want to answer it. That's where I was for most of my marriage, and it wasn't until 2017 (yes,16 years into marriage) that I chose to learn and explore more about how my body works in relation to sex. I was afraid of opening books, listening to advice, or even knowing the anatomy of my body because I thought I had to wade through smut to get there. I feared what I was going to find if I explored.

As I read and explored more about sex and then got in front of groups of woman to tell my story I began to think, *could my problem be the story I tell about the problem?* Hence this book was formed.

WHAT CHANGED MY PERCEPTION

1. WRITING OUT THOUGHTS, BELIEFS, AND FEELINGS ABOUT SEX

Pay attention to your emotions and be completely honest as you answer the following questions:

- How do I view sex?

- How do I feel about it?

- What do I think about the body, all parts of it?

- How did I first learn about sex?

- What was I taught?

- What do I really believe God feels about sex?

- How important is the sexual component of my marriage?

Schedule a time to share the answers you wrote with your spouse. Discuss what you've learned. Consider seeking professional help to work through any issues you may have uncovered.

2. WRITE DOWN THE BEST AND WORST ADVICE YOU RECEIVED ABOUT SEX.

I polled some women who have come to my trainings and asked them to share their best and worst advice about sex. You'll read some of their thoughts here.

WORST

It's my "job" to keep him happy even if I don't want to do it.

Worst advice was getting no advice.

Keep your expectations low. You'll probably be disappointed regardless.

Don't worry, it hurts a little. That's normal.

BEST

Your pleasure matters. You can tell your spouse exactly what you do or don't like.

That I need to figure out what works best for me.

Don't do anything you aren't comfortable with.

Communicate your feelings, and it's ok if you don't want to have sex.

What best or worst advice did you receive? What about your husband's advice that he got? Please take the time to add to this list and have a conversation about these.

3. UNDERSTANDING THE WHY'S OF SEX

Simply put, the why's of sex in marriage matter more than the what's of sex. Chastity isn't just about when sex happens; it's about why it happens. Let's hope that in marriage, sex will be shared for the right reasons, but that intention requires a deeper and fuller understanding of healthy sexuality.

Most couples receive little instruction about what good and healthy sex is and what that might mean in a marriage. At the end of the book I go into greater detail about the reasons why sex is important in marriage, but first I'd like you to write about and discuss with your husband what you think the "why" is behind sex for you.

4. YOU CAN BE A GOOD GIRL AND LEARN ABOUT SEX TOO

I've learned that being a good girl is a great thing. But good girls can read about, discuss and participate in marital sexual relations and still *be* good girls in the sight of God. Overcoming this syndrome does not mean that you become a bad girl, but rather that you develop a healthy and accurate understanding of the godly purposes and potential of sexual relations in marriage.

Ask for sacred help from a loving God. We know from *James 1:5* in the Bible that if any of us lacks wisdom, we can ask of God. So I did.

- Do you lack wisdom regarding sex within marriage?

- Do you lack wisdom regarding God's blessing upon sexual relations?

- Do you believe God will answer your questions regarding something such as sex?

He will! Why not seek a divine conviction of the godliness and holiness of sexual intimacy in marriage?

I was afraid to talk to God about sex. It was awkward to pray about, but when I recognized that God can be that physician and healer for me, I realized it was essential. He can and will heal you and make you whole, but He often does so with the help of friends, mentors, therapists, books, and other resources.

5. SEX IS GOOD AND COMES FROM GOD

Husband and wife must come to know that sex is good and of God. You must come to feel the divine permission, power, and potential of pure virtuous sexual relations within marriage--the way God designed them to be.

I knew sex was approved and necessary in marriage, but I didn't fully believe in it. After attending courses, classes, and reading dozens of books, I learned about the sanctity of sexual relations in my marriage, and I began to have a change of heart. I realized that sex was a vital aspect to a happy and healthy marriage. I acknowledged that sexual relations are approved by God and necessary to achieve the marital oneness I sought. This transformed my attitude, filled my heart with a renewed hope, and encouraged me to seek improvement in this area of my marriage.

You will begin to challenge and reprogram your deeply rooted beliefs and alter them to be completely aligned with how God feels about sexual relations in marriage. If you already have a healthy, vibrant belief that sex is good and blessed by God, then this information will fortify your faith.

Trust me, challenging old beliefs and gaining a firm conviction about the sanctity of sex will not immediately solve all sexual issues. But you've got to start somewhere. Working through some of the questions in this book will allow you to better understand what you're working with and what may be hindering you from a fulfilling, godly sexual relationship.

CHAPTER THREE

SEX IS FOR MY HUSBAND'S SATISFACTION

"He wants it...all...the...time."

Most men fall into that category (not all; we'll talk about that in Chapter Twelve, *"Why does my spouse want it so much more than me?"*).

Is it just because of their desire for the physical result of orgasm? Or are men just wild animals that are giving in to physical urges?

I used to believe both of those things. In fact, this is what I thought the definition of sex was:

The man has an orgasm.

There was a long time in our marriage when I believed that all I was to Trent was a body to have sex with. You've heard the phrase before, "lay like a dead fish?" Yeah, that's what I did. I didn't feel connected, and I didn't feel loved when we had sex.

Sex became a chore for me, something I had to tolerate for the sake of Trent. Babies and motherhood came along, and those became great excuses to put sex on the back burner on my "to do" list. I knew I had to have sex with Trent, so I would have the "check the box" sex and move on. I was really good at faking it too just to get him off of me sooner. I usually wasn't wanting to enjoy myself, and I felt Trent was just using my body for his pleasure, which led to resentment towards him.

I have talked with many women about this exact thing and found that they've all seen themselves not as someone who can choose and act, but as someone being acted upon.

Sex was an act that I didn't feel connected to in my own body because I had grown to despise it over time. I had so many negative thoughts about sex. Hearing the word or thinking about having to have sex felt toxic.

Were these accurate perceptions of Trent's feelings towards me or true statements about sex?

No.

They were perceptions defined by my own negative associations with and perception of sex.

I later learned that because of my own views on sex, I was not allowing myself to feel pleasure (and when I did, I felt guilt). I was accusing him of only having sex with me for the physical effects for him. I saw him as "selfish" for wanting to have sex with me...his wife!

Oh, the irony. I never want Trent to cheat on me, but I would resent him for wanting to have sex with me and make him feel bad about his desire to connect and physically express his love for me.

So many married women treat their husbands this way, not understanding what they are doing to their husbands who truly love them and want to connect with their wives. I know it's different for you who are in abusive relationships. Yes, not all men truly love and want to connect with their wives, but I've found that most do. They may not properly express it, and their anger and frustration from a lack of intimacy might make you feel like they don't love you. So before you give the final judgement, stay curious, and let's dive deeper.

One of the best resources I have found in understanding and relating to the man's perspective about how they view sex is the book, *For Women Only,* by Shaundi Feldhahn, a social researcher. Through interviews, focus groups and a detailed survey Shaunti attempts to explain the inner workings of a man's brain and why he does and says some of the things he does. The book sets out to help women understand and respect their husbands better.

Men, by nature, desire to have sex with women. Now I know this is not a new revelation, but this is important to understand a man's perspective. They are visually stimulated and therefore the natural man desires sex with women that they find attractive.

Good men realize they aren't animals and don't have to give in to these desires and urges, but instead choose to create a stable family life and get married.

An expectation in most marriages is that the spouses will be monogamous, but in exchange, there is also an expectation to connect sexually on a frequent basis. How frequent is totally up to the spouses. For some, that is 2-5 times a week. For others, it is 2-5 times a month or less.

The point is, men agree to overcome their natural desire to be with multiple women and instead choose to be with one woman. If they feel like they were conned and are now trapped in a marriage with little to no sexual connection, this sometimes can lead to infidelity--or at least a desire to get a divorce. This is *not* an excuse for or justification of men who cheat because they feel they aren't having enough sex. It is simply something to be aware of as we understand the nature of men and how they are wired.

Imagine now if I let this negative association to sex and feeling "used" progress to the point that I had sex just a few times a year with my husband. He would begin to feel unloved, unappreciated, and unwanted. If I start to reduce our sexual connection and block him from the thing we hold sacred, which we vowed to never share with any other person, it is understandable that he might feel like our marriage is coming to an end or might want out.

If you doubt your husband feels this way, and you can trust he will give you an honest answer, try asking him, *"Would it be possible for you to stay faithful and would our marriage last if we stopped having sex for a few years?"* Most healthy, adult men would probably say that this would at best put a major strain on your marriage and at worst lead to emotional and possibly physical infidelity and/or divorce. Sex has a binding affect on us. When it is taken away from a marriage, it does take a toll.

Of course, at that time of feeling like I was just being used for his sexual pleasure, if I had stopped having sex with Trent for a year or two and it in part led to him being unfaithful, I would have probably called him a "selfish pig". I would have felt that he had *finally* validated the beliefs which I had had the whole time about him only using sex like an animal, without any self-control.

Don't get me wrong. I'm not condoning adultery in any situation, *ever*, and I am not saying that in all cases women drive men to adultery as there truly are some pigs out there who have affairs out of pure selfishness. However, too many women do make their husbands feel powerless and emasculated for years and then are shocked when he breaks his vows and has an affair with another woman who makes him feel appreciated, wanted, and respected.

My belief is that as spouses in a marriage, we each contribute in some way to the marriage growing stronger or the marriage ending. There is rarely a clear answer as to a single thing that caused a marriage to end. It usually ends due to hundreds of little things that each spouse has or hasn't done and maybe one major event (like an affair) that people will want to point to and blame as the cause for divorce.

In my observation, a marriage where both spouses have a healthy view on sex and can communicate their wants and desires, the marriage seems to handle other obstacles with more ease. When they see sex as a unique, vulnerable way that they connect and share themselves with another human, it has more power to bind. Where they see sex as something not only for their spouse's satisfaction, but for themselves to enjoy too, the marriage tends to have a stronger bond.

In the audio course that Trent and I created, *Couples Connection Course*, we share and model how to have more authentic and vulnerable conversations around sex and what you and your spouse each want out of your sex life. These conversations may be hard at first, but out of them can come more connection, happiness, and a better sex life.

This belief that sex is just for men's satisfaction comes from old cultural traditions and other false beliefs. It sometimes can be caused by trauma or abuse. It can be created from past relationships where infidelity took part in the marriage ending. If this is how you currently see sex, that is okay. You can go from where you are now to eventually seeing sex as something powerful for you, and as something capable of creating a strong and healthy marriage partnership.

As women, I believe we have more power than most of us realize. Sex is powerful, as it can be used for expressing love and connection. It is also powerful because withholding sex from our spouse can diminish the feelings of connection and love, and in many cases create resentment. It also is used by some as a reward and punishment system, which often creates an unhealthy dynamic in a marriage.

Men have a lot of power too. When they treat their women with love, respect, and serve them in ways that are a sacrifice for them, they can motivate their wives to step out of their comfort zone and be more sexually adventurous and feel more desire to have sex.

Often, a man who feels like he is not having enough sex with his wife will show up as angry, resentful, bitter, and lacking the drive to work hard for his family. When he feels emasculated, unwanted, and unloved he may begin to sabotage his marriage. It is an emotionally immature way to react to these feelings, but it comes from poor modeling growing up or from not having proper communication skills to share these feelings with his spouse.

We see this play out in a selfish cycle. Wife isn't feeling loved, so she doesn't want to have sex with her husband. Husband is sexually frustrated from not having sex with his wife, so he treats his wife poorly and gets upset at the kids too. She feels less loved and emotionally distant and has even less desire to connect sexually. He becomes more bitter, angry and resentful and begins to sabotage his marriage and maybe even justify why he is enjoying the attention from that one woman at work. In the end, it is as if he is almost relieved to finally be divorced and free to explore the opportunity to find the "true" connection he desires from a woman who wants to be with him.

What is sad is that this cycle can be broken and divorce in many cases was not necessary and the problems that existed in that failed marriage will just carry on with those individuals in their next relationships unless something changes. If you and your husband find yourselves in this pattern of growing emotional and physical disconnect, resentment and bitterness, I hope you will both be loving and humble enough to see the other person's perspective.

Throughout the book there are questions and opportunities for conversations to understand more about how your spouse sees your sex life, what it means to them, and how it makes them feel. You will also have the opportunity to express what you desire from him to emotionally connect and you can share with him what he can do and how he can treat you to help increase your desire to sexually connect.

"SEX IS FOR MY HUSBAND'S SATISFACTION."

It isn't only for his satisfaction; to him, it is likely also for expressing love and admiration, and it is for connecting. To a good man, sex means more than just the pleasure or satisfaction he gets from the act.

I want all women who struggle with sex to know this. Sex is for you too. It is for your pleasure, your enjoyment, your connection, and for binding you and your spouse in a way that is sacred and unique.

Based on the name of this chapter, it may feel that I have taken you in a different direction than you expected. The rest of this book will help you to understand more ways that you can increase your desire and the enjoyment you receive from sex. It is not necessarily about sexual positions or specific actions. It starts with the conversations and emotional healing to prepare your mind and body to connect with your husband and receive pleasure. From experience I can tell you that being united as one in your relationship has a bigger impact on sexual satisfaction than trying new positions.

If your libido is low or you currently feel resentment towards your spouse because of their anger, their bitterness, something they've done, or how they treat you, please keep reading this book. Discover what things can increase your sexual confidence and desire as well as help you and your spouse uncover why there may be feelings of resentment or bitterness surrounding sex. My hope is that you can have conversations to overcome these negative feelings that may currently be a wedge in your marriage.

I now really enjoy having great, fully connected sex with Trent. My beliefs about sex have changed because I learned about my pleasure spots, how my body works, and am more curious about what I want to try and experience. So how did I come to this?

I started learning more about my body and the amazing, God-given arousal and pleasure points that women have. Trent and I started talking more about sex, and it became more comfortable. I taught Trent how to slow down and work on foreplay. I communicated what felt good, what I liked and what I didn't.

As you read this book, more questions will be presented, which as I mentioned before are designed to be *conversation starters*. They are topics and questions for you to talk about with your spouse. As you do, you will find out more about each other and possibly break down walls that have been hurting your marriage and this can make sex more desirable and more fun. You'll find out more about what you enjoy and what you don't. You may find that by allowing yourself to be curious and explore sex and pleasure within your marriage, you actually can enjoy it more. You have my permission!

WHAT CHANGED MY PERCEPTION

1. A WIFE'S RESPECT MEANS MORE TO A MAN THAN HER LOVE

My respect for Trent matters more to him than my love for him. Anger was Trent's way to show me he was feeling disrespected. Men would rather feel unloved than disrespected and inadequate. If they feel disrespected then they will feel unloved. They feel the pain and humiliation because of our disrespect. Men need to feel respected in order to feel loved.

How do wive's show respect to their husband's?

1. Respect his judgement by trusting his decisions

2. Respect his abilities especially when fixing things

3. Respect what he has accomplished

4. Respect in communication

5. Respect in public to those around you, brag about him!

6. Respect in our assumptions - no nagging

2. HUSBANDS NEED TO FEEL WANTED BY THEIR WIVES

I learned that for Trent, connecting sexually is much more than a physical act and having an orgasm. He can have an orgasm all alone if that's what he chooses, but that would just leave him empty and disconnected. For him, I've found that it is his primary way of emotionally connecting with me, and when I participate fully with him, with a desire to feel pleasure with him, he feels loved, appreciated, and--most importantly--wanted by me.

Husbands truly want to please their wives sexually. Ask any man. He wants his wife to experience orgasm, *every time*. While that may not be realistic, by simply wanting him and expressing desire to have sex with him, you are transforming him and creating a deeper connection.

3. MEN WANT TO CONNECT EMOTIONALLY, BUT THEY OFTEN DON'T KNOW HOW TO DO THAT OUTSIDE OF SEX

Once I understood how simple Trent's view of sex with me was and how deeply he wanted to emotionally connect with me that way, I became more interested in having sex with him. Of course, there were many other things which we both had to change to get to that point. I had to examine my beliefs about sex, and he had to work on showing me love the way I most appreciate it; through acts of service. (Trent is the best at doing dishes and also cooks dinner more than I do because he knows I don't enjoy those things.)

If you don't know your love language or your husband's please take the time to go take the free test now at www.5lovelanguages.com. I'll talk more about this later in Chapter Eight.

4. MAKING YOUR MAN FEEL LIKE A MAN

I realized most good men are really simple. We women are the complicated ones. If you don't believe that your husband feels this way, ask him the following questions about sex (assuming you are both honest with each other and actually can talk about sex. If not, continue on in the book and we'll help you get there):

If I initiate sex and tell you how bad I want you, does that make sex more enjoyable than just laying there and letting you use my body?

When I have sex with you and I am totally involved and wanting you to please me with your body, how does that make you feel as my man?

When I want you to feel pleasure by regularly connecting our bodies and hearts through sex, how does that motivate you in other areas of your life, such as work? Do you feel more or less desire to serve me and spend time with me?

Believe me. I've never heard back from any woman that her man would prefer she just lay there. Making your man feel like a man, in the way he desires it most, will change your husband.

5. HUSBANDS WANT THEIR WIVES

Men (I mean real men; there are some dirt bags out there and this doesn't apply to them) do not want to sleep with another woman. Sure, men are visual, and they have a hard time not appreciating attractive people, but they do not want to be with another woman and they do not want someone else. They want their wives.

Remember, your husband chose you. Men frequently share with my husband and I that as long as they feel that their wives want them (sexually) and express their love and appreciation in the way they prefer to receive it (usually through sex and positive words), then they would go to war for them. They will cherish and serve their wives in any way they are asked. Real men want just one sexy (to them), confident woman, and they truly desire to be wanted by that woman. If they have that, men are happy, driven, and become warriors for their wives. If they don't feel wanted or appreciated by their wives, men feel emasculated, frustrated, angry, and can easily be irritated.

Men still have the same responsibility they have always had: to love and serve their wives without expecting anything in return. As they love and cherish their wives, work to provide for them and invest time with their children, it is my hope that their wives will love and cherish them and connect with them in a way that makes their men *feel* loved, appreciated and wanted through great, fully involved, and fully connected sex.

Here is my new definition of sex, which you will get to experience much more often when you choose it:

My goal is that as you go through this book, you will be able to break down walls and have open conversations about sex with your spouse, and that you will be on your way to better sex, better connection, and a better marriage.

CHAPTER FOUR

SHAME KILLS LOVE

Sexual shame is the silent killer of sex lives. The phrase *shame kills love* comes from Kristin Hodson, *LCSW, CST*, Instagram account (@kristinbhodson). She says that, *"shame kills love"* Kristin has some incredible sexual health information in her Instagram feed that will add a lot of value to not only your marriage but your family. Be sure to go follow her. The goal of her Instagram account is to help you become the sex expert in your life and to be able to share it with your children so you can teach them about their sexuality when appropriate.

> *"As a therapist and in my daily interactions with people, I see shame as a soul-eating emotion. I see so many different sexual problems and at the root of so many of them is deep-seated sexual shame."*
>
> --Kristin Hodson, LCSW, CST

Whether you came upon sexual shame through religious programming, sexual abuse, manipulative ex-partners who damaged your self-esteem, or any other reason, sexual shame is a common and unfortunate byproduct of being raised in a world with a lot of harmful and unproductive views on sexuality.

Whatever the root cause of your sexual shame, know that it can be overcome.

Sexual shame (or shame of any kind) is not our natural state. It is not in our nature to feel ashamed of who we are as human beings. God didn't design us that way. We are not born ashamed of ourselves. Sexual shame is a learned behavior from our environment and situations we are in throughout life.

I'd like to share with you a quick visual model that I came across by Jordan Gray, a *Sex & Relationship Coach.* He illustrates the overall journey that you're going to be embarking on.

We are born as beautiful, innocent little blank slates. Hardwired into our bodies is the fact that we are sexual beings.

At a certain point in our upbringings, we start to receive unhelpful messages about sexuality, and how we should feel about sex. These can include:

– Good girls don't like sex

– Men only want one thing from women

– God won't love you if you _____ (fill in the blank with your own belief about sex)

– You can't be sexually attractive if you are the way you are (too short/tall/fat/skinny, etc.)

I could go on, but you get the point.

What these messages do is start to create doubt within ourselves, which leads to feeling ashamed of our sexuality.

We hear through our culture that you shouldn't be too sexual (or sexual at all). We are sexual beings, so we ourselves feel wrong, unlovable, disgusting, evil, etc. This wraps a layer of shame around our sexuality.

The inconsistency between a belief that we shouldn't be too sexual or shouldn't want sex and our natural desire for sex is where sexual shame originates and it begins to hurt us. Maybe we have been told at a young age that being sexually aroused is wrong/evil/bad, and yet we still feel sexual urges (because that's simply what bodies do when around others we are sexually attracted to), and so this makes us feel wrong/evil/bad.

Sexual shame can be a vicious cycle. Ultimately (because the opposite of shame is innocence), the only way out of this cycle is to overpower our sexual shame with love and acceptance.

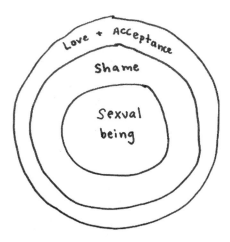

Nothing heals without love. We must drown out the sexual shame and guilt with love and acceptance until the shame dwindles to nothing.

"You slowly, step-by-step, re-experience the old stimulus that once caused you the negative emotion, and you consciously re-experience it in a safer context, until the negative emotional charge no longer associates with the core issue. It is often said that "neurons that fire together, wire together." And so because your sexual response wired to something that is less than desirable, the way to move past this stage is to attach it to something that you want it to be associated with (i.e. love, ease, and acceptance, instead of shame, guilt, fear, or anxiety)."

--Jordan Gray, Sex & Relationship Coach

With patience, persistence, and self-compassion, love will eventually drown out the sexual shame and replace it if you are intentional about it.

WHAT CHANGED MY PERCEPTION

1. IDENTIFYING THE ROOT ISSUE

While you don't want to spend too much time on this point, becoming aware of and directly naming the source of the majority of your sexual shame is a beneficial step to go through. I will mention some common sources of sexual shame throughout this book.

Maybe it was a religious upbringing, a shaming spouse, or one of your parents who did the majority of the damage to your relationship with your sexuality. Who or whatever it was, remember what brought you to this point of sexual shame in the first place.

It's okay to honor the feelings that come up.

In naming the root issue of your sexual shame directly, it's not uncommon for there to be some emotional residue attached to your shame sources.

You might feel sad and want to mourn the lost years of your sex life. You might feel angry or personally victimized. You may feel hurt. Whatever is there to feel, feel it fully.

2. UNDERSTAND SHAME VERSUS GUILT

Brené Brown likes to call herself "the shame researcher." She has spent the past two decades studying courage, vulnerability, shame, and empathy.

From one of her many remarkable life changing books, *Daring Greatly*, she defines shame as: *"the intensely painful feeling or experience of believing that we are flawed, and therefore unworthy of love and belonging."*

Then, from her famous TED talk she shares:

> *"Shame is a focus on self; guilt is a focus on behavior. Shame is "I am bad." Guilt is "I did something bad." How many of you, if you did something that was hurtful to me, would be willing to say, "I'm sorry. I made a mistake"? How many of you would be willing to say that? Guilt: I'm sorry. I made a mistake. Shame: I'm sorry. I am a mistake."*
>
> --Brené Brown, Author & Research Professor

For Brown, guilt is what we feel when we do something bad, and it can motivate us to change. By contrast, shame is what we feel when we think we are bad, and it doesn't motivate us to change. It just makes us feel horrible.

Brown writes that the opposite of shame is empathy and self-compassion, and that's true.

What has been your experience with the word *shame*? Let us know and understand the differences between these two words to make the lasting change we want to see in our lives and those around us.

3. I CAN HEAL FROM MY SEXUAL SHAME / TRAUMA

Whatever messages you received about sex (from society, church, family, etc.), it isn't your fault that you received those messages. But it is your responsibility to step up to the plate and do your own individual healing work.

I decided to dig a little deeper into my own healing. I took an eight-week Prana course along with other women. The course teaches you to reconnect with your body, and develop deep self-compassion that transforms the way you talk and think about yourself. The course is taught by a dear friend of mine, Sariah Bastian. In this course, we learned about how our mind can be used as a tool to go inside and observe the body that we live in.

In life we have so many tools to explore and observe the outer world, but we are not properly taught how to go inside ourselves and observe our own inner world.

In Sariah's book, Beyond Breath, she shares, *"the chakra system is the program you unconsciously run; it's how you react to life. There are seven chakras, each associated with a nerve bundle tied to different parts of your body through which your body speaks to you."*

The second chakra specifically deals with emotional intelligence. It is located in the sacrum which is connected to your hips, lower back, genitals, abdomen, kidneys, bladder and reproductive system. When we feel tight in these areas of the body, your emotional intelligence is telling you that there is a problem. Below are a few questions that Sariah uses to help you observe and recognize how you give and receive emotions, connection, intimacy, and sexuality, and where this feedback is coming from that something is off.

In Sariah's book she asks these questions about the second chakra:

> *"Can you feel deeply without dousing those around you in your emotional waters? Do you fear hurting others because of the way you feel? Are you able to experience passion and intimacy with another? Are you comfortable moving your body? Do you know you have the right to feel?"*
> --Sariah Bastian, author of *Beyond Breath*

At times, we go through life living the same patterns and not recognizing what's happening within our bodies. Many times throughout my first 16 years of marriage, I would beat myself up and ask myself negative questions like, "what's wrong with me? Why is sex so difficult for me?"

When I went through the Prana course, I was able to observe my past belief systems that I was acting on and the actions and behaviors I was living in. It kept me stuck in the same place, where I was having the same experiences over and over again.

This course taught me to learn to trust myself and hold myself in safety wherever I went, and to observe the different parts of my body because they were speaking to me through feedback in the different chakras. I didn't necessarily have deep trauma around my sexuality or betrayal trauma due to my spouse or former relationships like other women in my group did, but I was able to learn from their trauma and what they shared. If you feel that you need this support, I suggest enrolling in one of Sariah's live or online courses. To learn more, go to sariahbastian.com

4. AN ANTIDOTE TO SEXUAL SHAME

My way of moving through these feelings was with immense *curiosity* and *compassion*. Both have been my antidote to sexual shame. At the core, I view curiosity as the emotion that helps us expand our understanding of ourselves and the world in which we live in (i.e. curiosity to live abroad, to try new foods, to learn a new language, and to meet new people).

As children, we have an innate curiosity about life that we surely lose as we move into adulthood. The beauty of curiosity is that it continuously informs our next step forward. Once we've experienced that situation or behavior, we can consciously choose whether to repeat it or not.

Compassion is the voice of your best friend, who whispers "you are enough" at every turn. Recently there has been some breakthrough research done on self-compassion by a social psychologist Kristin Neff from the University of Texas at Austin. Among other things, Neff discovered that self-compassion can act as an antidote to self-criticism—a major characteristic of those who experience intense shame. It was found that self-compassion is a powerful trigger for the release of oxytocin, the hormone that increases feelings of trust, calm, safety, generosity, and connectedness.

When all is said and done, moving into uncharted waters will only inform our paths, and no matter the outcome, we are *always* enough as we already are.

5. ALLOWING MY HUSBAND TO HELP ME MOVE TO THE NEXT LAYER OF LOVE AND SELF-ACCEPTANCE

There's only so much healing we can do on our own. Your husband should be someone you feel safe with, and as you continue to read, communication is key. Let your spouse in on your process. Tell them what you're working through, and be explicit in telling them how they can best help you through it.

It can be as simple as saying, "I'm working on feeling safe in my body during sex, so I would love if you could give me extra reassurance and tenderness when we're making love. Look me in the eyes a lot. Be present with me. Tell me you love me and that I'm safe. Stuff like that. Can you do that for me? It would help a lot."

Sharing clearly and deliberately will help you to heal your sexual shame faster than trying to engage in vague, mind-reading sex. That's what a lot of women dealing with shame have done for years and nothing has changed. We get to choose to do things differently so the outcome will change.

6. PRACTICE PATIENCE, SELF-COMPASSION, AND HAVE A SENSE OF HUMOR

Sexual shame doesn't shift 100% overnight. Like anything worth having in life, this process will take time and consistent effort.

Make sure that you remain kind to yourself in your inner dialogue as you're chipping away at your sexual shame. You're overcoming years (or decades...or generations) of negative sexual programming, and you are not expected to arrive at a place of healing in one or two experiences.

Remember that you are also allowed to experience an array of emotional content as you're working through your sexual shame. You might cry (yes, I did a bit of crying myself). You might get angry. You may laugh (I hope you laugh).

It's all welcome. All of it. Let the energy move through you. It hasn't had a voice for so long, and it wants to heal through your expressiveness.

7. HEAL YOUR PERSONAL SEXUAL RELATIONSHIP FIRST

"When coming to know what God gave me, masturbation is unapologetically good."
--Jennifer Finlayson-Fife, Ph.D.

Learning about masturbation has given me an opportunity to educate myself and confront and identify my own biases, values, fears and judgements towards it. As a young woman, I don't think I understood what masturbation was. I believe I was in my 20s before I realized people manually stimulated themselves to orgasm (yes, I was that innocent through my teenage years).

I've learned that our sexuality is an inherent, God-given part of who we are, from the moment we are born to the moment we die. Understanding our sexuality and learning to express and manage our sexuality is an important part of developing a healthy sexual agency.

Because the messages I received growing up were that you shouldn't touch your private parts, the only time I touched my vulva was to quickly wash it and try to avoid and suppress any feelings of arousal.

I have come to believe that knowing my own body-- my likes and dislikes--can help my intimate life in many ways. If you're open to it, masturbation is one way of figuring out what you would like to experience so you can express to your husband what you would like or what he can do for you to increase your pleasure during sex.

Honestly, masturbation is still something that I have not fully explored. I have not felt much need to as by the time I started researching it, I was well on my way to a much better sex life and communication with Trent. I knew what I did and didn't like and can climax quicker than he can most of the time. I have only experimented with masturbation a few times and I personally felt more comfortable that my husband was with me. Some women have expressed that they would be more comfortable trying this alone. That is a great conversation to have with your husband to decide if that is something you want to explore and how that will work.

Some men are aroused by watching their wife show him what feels good to her. Other men feel threatened by it. You will have to discuss that with your spouse and if he feels threatened, ask questions with curiosity as to what he fears. Few women, if any, prefer practicing masturbation to having sex with their husband. The act of connecting through sex isn't replaced by masturbation.

Medical science does not support the belief that physical or mental harm comes from masturbation as was once taught in the late 1800s or early 1900s. Studies do however show significant harm from excessive shame, fear, and aversion to sexual feelings.

When I first started studying this topic, I wanted to have the opportunity to look at the information and decide consciously where this fits for me and my family rather than simply doing what most parents do: not even talk about it. I also didn't want to let my fears steer my ship when it comes to teaching my children about their sexuality.

Masturbation is a normal behavior. When you shame it, you're taking something normal, and you're making people feel less worthy of love and acceptance from God. Masturbation can be used negatively. If it is habitually used as a coping mechanism or if it is used simply to indulge in lust and fantasy, it can lead to other undesirable behaviors. I think this is why most people take the hard line approach of, "masturbation is bad in all cases and in all situations".

Sex therapists consistently recommend women who have a hard time feeling sensation during intercourse to practice masturbation. This allows them to learn to feel their vulva, vagina and clitoris. To understand what feels good so they can learn to focus on those sensations and try different positions with their spouse to improve their sexual experiences.

This shame associated with masturbation can often be the main cause of a repetitive cycles of acting out when an individual uses it as a coping mechanism.

Let's say an individual is trying to cope with something difficult in their life and uses masturbation along with fantasy or pornography (A.K.A. they're acting out). Because of beliefs that this is wrong, they feel shame. This creates self-loathing, which triggers more acting out. This cycle repeats itself as the individual's self worth sinks lower.

Shame is not how we help someone break an unhealthy coping mechanism. Just as fat-shaming has a low success rate at curing obesity, so does shaming those who use masturbation as a coping mechanism have a low success rate at changing the behavior.

I believe that masturbation can be used as a tool to improve intimacy, as it is prescribed by sex therapists to help some women (and men) to better understand and explore their bodies and learn more about how to feel pleasure. I also believe it can be used in a negative way as is the case when someone uses it as a sexual release instead of connecting with their spouse. I have heard from some women that their husbands no longer want to have sex with them and in many cases, they later discover their husband has been masturbating to pornography instead. One common reason was they didn't feel connected to their wife and found masturbation *easier* than working on the relationship in order to increase the frequency of sex with their spouse.

This topic requires a lot of thought and maybe several deep conversations to determine what part this does or doesn't play in your marriage. Some decide solo masturbation is ok when it is communicated to the other spouse. Others have determined to use it only as part of their sex while they are together. While some have decided to completely exclude it from their marriage. Consider the following in your discussion.

"I understand that like any normal human tendency, masturbation can become an unhealthy behavior. This is also true for eating – yet we don't couch our physical desire to nourish ourselves with food as sinful. I believe it is unhealthy for masturbation to be done in a way which interferes with your daily functioning or quality of relationships. I do not want to minimize this for those who have struggled or who have suffered in a marriage where their spouse has withdrawn sexually in part because of an unhealthy masturbation habit.

At the same time, I believe unnecessary masturbatory shame and unmet attachment needs are at the core of most compulsive masturbatory behavior – becoming an unhealthy coping skill used in times of stress and discontent."

--Natasha Helfer Parker, LCMFT, CST, CSTS

This is all the more reason to confront your ideas surrounding masturbation and learn how to become comfortable with these topics. You don't need to explore masturbation if you choose not to. Involve God in the process of cultivating, appreciating, and mastering, and not removing, suppressing, or rejecting sexual desire.

I am choosing to neither condone nor condemn, but simply provide information and guidance, as you would with any other important topic. Remain curious as you discuss your history and beliefs about this and listen to understand your spouse's perspective if it differs from your own. Try to keep your conversation free of shame as you determine how to improve sexual connection and strengthen your marriage.

CHAPTER FIVE

I SHOULDN'T LEARN ABOUT SEX

The summer of 2017, our family of seven was on a five week, four country trip through Central America. We had left our home in Utah a couple of weeks before we arrived in Guatemala. We rented a home in a little compound of five houses on the edge of Lake Atitlán in Panajachel, Guatemala. It just so happens that in the same compound there was another family of seven, also from Utah, that would be there the entire 10 days we would be.

Small world, right?

Our families didn't have any plans, so we just relaxed together on a lazy Sunday afternoon. Suzanne (an amazing mom of five) and I hit it off right away, and spent the whole afternoon our first day there getting to know each other.

As our conversation turned more personal, we opened up to each other about our past and our beliefs around sex and intimacy in marriage. She basically shared that a year previously she was where I was in my beliefs and thinking about sex and intimacy. I asked her what made her decide to change and what helped her change her heart and mind. She simply said, "*I just wanted to be awesome at sex.*"

I thought to myself in that moment, "Why would you want that?" I didn't desire sex, and I didn't talk about sex (except with Trent on rare occasions), so it blew my mind that someone wanted to do all that hard work in order to change.

Suzanne started her journey because she had always been a fan of romance novels but was disappointed because it didn't flow into her real life. She discovered that she wanted sex more than the romance she had been craving. She did warn me that as she began to learn about sex she was afraid to pursue it because of family members who had struggled with sexual addictions, but she was desperate.

I cannot tell you how much I related to her in that moment. No, I'm not a fan of romance novels, but chick flicks can do the same for me. She gave me permission to explore this topic of sex and intimacy without shame.

Our families ended up spending most of the next nine days together, eating, participating in various activities, and serving at our favorite charity. (*Cultiva International*--seriously, check them out). My heart softened after many conversations, and I began to see her point of view, and why she wanted to be awesome at sex.

I finally surrendered.

For years, Trent tried to get me to talk more and learn more about sex. We had multiple discussions about why I thought the way I did about sex, and why I never seemed to want it. These conversations always seemed to end in frustration for both of us. Up to this point in our marriage, most of our arguments were about sex--not money but sex.

After just a few days with Suzanne, I made more progress in opening my mind to the idea that I could learn about sex, and be good at sex, than I had made from 16 years of discussions with Trent. Sometimes women just need to talk to women.

WHY DO WOMEN FEEL THEY NEED PERMISSION TO LEARN ABOUT THEIR BODIES?

I chose to listen to this new friend whom I had just met and came to trust very quickly. It was as if I finally received permission from someone who wasn't my husband. (All those years I assumed his intentions for getting me to learn more about sex were purely selfish--to just get more sex).

Receiving this permission from another woman who had struggled with sex too was important to me. I felt motivated by her story of overcoming her hang-ups with sex and how she spoke so positively about it. That made me realize there was hope for me too.

It didn't register until Suzanne encouraged me to learn more about my body and it's sexual capabilities. For years I was waiting for someone else (who was not my husband) to tell me it was okay to learn more about my body and sex. I was waiting for approval from an outside source, whom I trusted and didn't seem to have ulterior motives, before I could learn about my genitals, to understand what turns me on and why.

Because of the culture and environment I grew up in, I felt like I wasn't able to explore or understand my body. I didn't talk about sex, about the vulva or vagina, and I didn't even know what a clitoris was for the first several years being married. I even thought I only had two holes in my pelvic area (the answer is there are three). I just assumed looking at, touching, or thinking about my sexual organs would suddenly make me a "bad girl."

I want to tell you: you are not a bad girl. You are a sexual being with sexual needs and desires that are God-given. You have His permission to learn about one of the greatest gifts He has given you: your body, your power to procreate, and your ability to connect at the deepest emotional, physical, and even spiritual levels through sex with your spouse.

If you are like me, you have suppressed, pushed down, hidden, shamed, and ignored any thoughts about sex, or desire for sex or pleasure, and have created patterns that suppress your sexuality. While those patterns may have served you when you were single and wanting to abstain from sex, they now cause issues in your marriage when your spouse wants to bond with you. Your spouse may not have ever expressed that to you, but I've found that many good men are afraid to hurt their wife's feelings, so they don't express how that lack of intimacy or lack of connection through sex is affecting them.

- You have permission to read books about your sexual organs.

- You have permission to read books about arousal and how the female brain works.

- You have permission to open up to receive more pleasure during sex with your husband.

- You have permission to ask for what your husband can do to turn you on to get you ready for sex (First you need to figure this out yourself. Chapter Eight, *The Female Sexual Response Cycle,* can help you figure out what works for you).

- You have permission to be selfish in sex, to enjoy sex and orgasm without shame or guilt.

I want you to take this permission and begin your journey. You don't need to do so with reckless abandon. Take small steps and read some of the books I have on my bookshelf. I would highly recommend reading at least the first six listed.

Text the word **RESOURCES** to **801-505-9750**, and you'll get a link to my up-to-date reading list (I'm always adding to it) and other great resources.

Begin having conversations with your husband about what you want. As you learn how he can better turn you on and how he can help you reach orgasm, express that to him. He *wants* to please you. It sounds silly to you and me, but men feel so empowered, so turned on, and so manly when they know they have the power to turn you on and to help you climax during sex. Allow him to do that by sharing with him what you are learning and what you want to try.

My goal here is to help you become aware that there is a lot that you can do to make your sexual experience both more fulfilling and more pleasurable. The more you know about what can change and what you can add to your experience, the more in control and empowered you will feel.

That is what learning about sex can do for you, too. It can open all the doors of your life when you stop resisting it, pushing it down and pretending it isn't there.

I never thought of myself as a sexual person. But after having these conversations with Suzanne I realized and came to the conclusion that I too wanted to be great at sex, and that I could be more sexual, so I did. Look where I am now--writing a book about sex two years later. My life has completely changed because I chose to surrender and allow myself the honor of being in control of my sexual life.

WHAT CHANGED MY PERCEPTION

1. GIVING YOURSELF PERMISSION

Well, after well over a decade of this, I was done playing the good girl! I knew I needed to challenge my beliefs around my sexuality. I had several long conversations with Suzanne, who had been in the same place I was in. She began to guide me on where I could go to learn more in a safe way. In essence, I felt like someone else was giving me permission to finally learn and overcome the fear I held on to around learning about sex. So, I read and read. I allowed myself that permission to learn about *me* and how my body works in relation to arousal and sex.

I came across this quote that started me on a wonderful new view:

"You have God's permission to enjoy sex within your marriage. He invented sex; He thought it up to begin with. You can learn to enjoy it, and can develop a thrilling, happy marriage."
--Ed Wheat, Author of Intended for Pleasure

2. COURAGE TO SHARE YOUR STORY

Sometimes all we need is a gentle push to open up and share our story, feelings, or experiences. But in order to do that, you must find something essential: courage. You need courage to talk about it and courage to give yourself permission to be sexual.

I never thought I would be teaching women about their bodies and helping them navigate their sexual lives. But I wanted other women to be aware that they can escape from suffering in their silence and finding no hope because they don't want to talk about it. So that propelled me to share my story.

I made a choice to see things others did not see. I chose to believe things others did not believe. I've said things others could not say. I've done things others don't do. And I've received things others have yet to receive because I was willing to share.

Since making this choice to jump all in and teach and educate on sexuality my journey has been liberating. I think courage has a lot of power and influence that you may not realize until you do it for yourself. You don't need to open up to a bunch of women but find the courage to share to a few close trusted friends to see if there's any common ground among you. You never know until you open your mouth.

3. START READING AND EDUCATING YOURSELF

The first book I read when I chose to start researching sex was *Come As You Are* by Emily Nagoski. If you were to only read *one* book, I highly suggest this one. The biggest takeaway I walked away with in that book was the garden metaphor. This metaphor *literally* changed my whole mindset with this visual. To summarize, it goes something like this:

Your mind is like a garden. This garden has lots of space for growing amazing things. As time goes on the people around you start to plant their views, language and attitudes and ideas around your body, sex, and relationships in your garden.

As you go through adolescence, you are given the opportunity to take over your garden. You notice that some things that were planted in your garden are pretty toxic crap. So now you find yourself in a position analyzing each spot of your garden, figuring out what you want to keep and nurture and what you want to replace.

Some were lucky enough that their gardens were planted with some pretty healthy stuff. But some of us were not so lucky and end up with years of excavation because of the toxic crap.

It's time to rescue those limp and strangled plants. Not all plants grow equally well in all soils, and some plants deplete or enrich the soil in which they grow. If you plant a bad idea in temperamentally resistant soil, the idea won't take root. In contrast, if you plant a dangerous idea, it could not only take root but strangle other plants and drain even the most resilient of soils of its nutrients. If you dig up that plant, your options for replanting there are limited by the need to replenish the soul.

You get to choose whether or not to continue judging or fearing. You get to decide whether to leave that stuff in your garden or uproot it! It's not an infinite range of choice, but it *is* a choice.

Sometimes people need help in their garden. And I pray this book will help you look at your garden more deeply. Sometimes you want to fix someone else's garden for them. Unfortunately, you can't do that. And sometimes other people want to come tell you how to fix your garden. Sometimes it's their business; often it's not.

Education is power, girls! I promise that as you educate yourself, you will feel empowered to become the sex expert in *your* life. I know that for myself, and I just encourage you to seek the truth and tend to your garden through reading, understanding, and listening.

4. FIND YOUR COMFORT ZONE AROUND SEX

When women give themselves permission to be sexual, they have the key to finding and defining their comfort zone. You can learn to give yourself permission to value and honor this important part of who you are.

In order to find your comfort zone around sex, you must first give yourself permission to learn about yourself. What do I mean exactly by finding your comfort zone? I mean feeling at ease with your sexual needs and desires; feeling comfortable in your own skin; feeling comfortable talking about your sexuality with your spouse and advocating for protection and practicing safe sex; and feeling comfortable finding out how to take care of your sexual health.

I am fully aware that talking about sex can feel uncomfortable, but it doesn't have to feel that way. In fact, if we take the subject from behind closed doors and treat it with respect and the care it deserves, we will do ourselves a big favor.

We will get much closer to one of my goals along with many others in this field of teaching human sexuality: to make sex--and talking about sex--a *natural* part of life--something completely normal, special and fun. I want my children to hear about it in normal, safe, age-appropriate conversations in my home. I want them to know what source they can turn to with questions so their curiosity doesn't lead them to unsafe places to find answers.

I believe that by making sex an approachable, natural subject worthy of a conversation, we can show women how much they can gain from becoming more comfortable around the topic. I want them--and you--to know that the more you learn about your own body and how you respond to stimulation, the more you will feel grounded, satisfied, and fulfilled in your life.

Finding your comfort zone around sex is about knowing your boundaries and limits. Never let anyone pressure you to do or try something that makes you feel uncomfortable. And don't let a spouse make you feel guilty. Sex is something to engage in respectfully.

I've found that I'm now willing to try new things that I wouldn't have years ago. Trent and I have slowly attempted different things, and I've become more comfortable with my body. I know that I can have a safe conversation where my desires are respected. If there is something we try and I don't like it, I can verbalize that.

5. SEX NEEDS TO BE TAKEN OUT OF THE DARKNESS AND BROUGHT INTO LIGHT

I want to share with you an analogy that my friend Suzanne shared about the closet of sexuality. She has given me permission to use this here in my book and I'm excited to share it with you.

"Imagine that sex and sexuality is like a dark closet. While growing up, you may have been told to avoid the closet until you are older or married, and for some of you even mentioning "the closet" was taboo.

As you grow older, you see a variety of outcomes for those who enter the closet. Some women go in the closet and come out with an untimely pregnancy, feel ashamed, dirty, addicted to porn or masturbation, feel abused, while those who say they love it and express their excitement for the dark closet are considered to lack virtue or goodness.

For those who are married or in a relationship add it to their list of duties, like doing the laundry or taking care of the kids, as being a good wife or spouse. Very few seem to enjoy it, much less talk about it.

When it's your turn to go in, your parents may have given you a book to read to prepare you or have a talk with you; but when you enter the closet the lights are off and you feel woefully unprepared. You spouse is very excited about it and wonders why you aren't. Because you don't have many positive reviews on the dark closet of sex and sexuality; and your interest in the closet doesn't match your spouse; you feel broken and the pressure to engage creates a space of pain or resentment between your spouse and yourself. You've been warned to not turn on the lights because you'll see things that will enslave you, corrupt you, or you'll learn about things that you anticipate will gross you out.

So, every time you enter the closet, you stumble around and may learn a few things that are helpful; but you can't seem to shake the pain and resentment of feeling inadequate about your sexuality and sex. When and why you turn on the light of the dark closet is up to you.

When you do choose to turn on the lights, what you find will be a broad spectrum of information. Some of it will not appeal to you at all; some will make you feel dirty because of how you were taught to think about your body and sexuality while growing up; some of it will excite you and make you realize that you actually like sex; and that all the things that you wouldn't allow yourself to consider before you entered the dark closet can actually help you understand your body, a divine creation, and feel a deeper connection with your spouse.

It's important to realize that you are not a bad person for turning on the lights. Just because you are aware of the contents of the dark closet of sex and sexuality, and even explored some of those contents doesn't make you a bad person. You are learning about the most potent way to connect with another human being that is sanctioned by God."

6. JUDGEMENT VS CURIOSITY

As a Christian woman, I didn't know where to turn to find ways to "spice up" my sex life. I didn't want to find myself down a rabbit hole in the internet, exposing my eyes to ideas that would make me feel like a bad girl. I surely didn't want to ask my friends about it either, and definitely not my sisters. I was a lost woman with no hope.

Trent was the one who would present different ideas, and I would immediately judge him for it. He was personally looking for ways to please me, but I took it as something he did without my permission.

Some women operate outside their comfort zone because they simply never learned enough about sex and were taught that "good girls" should not be curious about it. Others, like myself, married young and quickly had children, and they never bothered or found the time to investigate this side of themselves.

I want you to come to the realization that curiosity is healthy and necessary--it's not only a goal but also an attitude that will uncover so many wonderful things during the course of your life.

Curiosity is the direct line to your soul!
It's begging you for growth.

Most of us, in fact, let life get in the way of connecting sexually and intimately. We push it to the bottom of our "to do" list, or maybe it wasn't even on our list to begin with. By the time we know we haven't connected for a while, we are too tired or distracted to even open the door to the possibilities of what that connection can do for us. Besides, we tend to go to our old habits, patterns, and positions to get the job done. After a while--or maybe a short while--sex gets, well...*boring.*

Doing the same thing over and over again whether in the bedroom or not can get mundane and not exciting anymore. I thrive on change everywhere *but* the bedroom. That's my personality. But it doesn't have to be that way; when you drop the judgement of what you've been told what sex is, possibility and curiosity open themselves to you.

Curiosity begins when you let go of what sex and intimacy is supposed to look like. The number one complaint that I hear from couples about their sex life is that it is boring. The spark died, the deep longing look into each other's eyes faded. But it doesn't have to be that way. Make the choice now to look at another angle and see other's perspectives on this God-given gift of sex. It's okay to be curious, to learn and read about sex. Educating yourself is an opportunity to let yourself enjoy sex and therefore be closer to your spouse.

CHAPTER SIX

I'M NOT THAT GREAT IN BED

There have been times when I was not very comfortable with what Trent expected of me, especially in the beginning of our marriage. I didn't always feel like I had control over our sexual relationship. It was stressful and I worried about it frequently.

Did you know that you can have a habit of worrying? I would worry about if I was doing enough for my husband to keep him happy. I would worry about what my body looked like in the light. I even used to worry about my performance inside and outside of the bedroom. I would worry about the facial expressions I would give while we made love. Or worrying about the position of my pelvic floor for him so it was pleasurable enough.

I found that I'd created that habit, but the good news is that there is a way to end it. Worrying for some of us is a default setting our minds go to when we aren't paying attention.

Trent and I went to Guatemala a second time about seven months after taking our family. As part of our trip, we were going ocean fishing near Iztapa, Guatemala. I worried about that trip because I had a fear of the ocean.

I had recently learned a trick by one of my favorite mentors, Mel Robbins. I learned that fear and excitement are actually the same feeling. Part of overcoming this fear of the ocean was to trick my mind into believing that I was excited to go fishing.

I gave myself a pep talk the whole drive over to the marina. I told myself that I was excited to go fishing, and I visualized myself catching a huge fish! As I got into the boat, I could just about hear my heart beating through my chest.

We began our journey out into the wide-open ocean; I started using that mind trick over and over again. I would say in my mind, "I'm excited, I'm excited, I'm excited." I heard the fisherman say, "I got one." It was my turn to come to the edge of the boat to hold the pole and to reel in the fish and tug on the line. I wrestled that fish for about 5 minutes. I wanted to give up because I was worn out, but I continued and as it turns out, I did catch that fish. A six foot long sailfish!

When your mind takes you somewhere sad, dark, doubtful, or negative you don't have to go with it. Now when I start feeling anxious or start to worry, I choose to ask myself two questions:

- What am I grateful for in this moment?

- What do I want to remember?

It forces me to focus on the positive aspects of my life. As soon as I do, I start to feel grateful instead of worried. So, as I began my journey of discovery, I was scared about what I was going to find and worried that I wouldn't get the answers I was looking for.

> *"It's okay to be scared. Being scared means you're about to do something really, really brave!"*
> --Mel Robbins, Author of *The 5 Second Rule*

Anxiety is what happens when your habit of worrying spirals out of control. The key to beating anxiety is to understand it. If you can catch it and reframe it, you'll stabilize your thoughts before your mind escalates into a full-blown panic.

Excitement and anxiety or fear feel the same way in your body. The only difference between excitement and anxiety or fear is what your mind calls it.

I've tricked my mind to feel the same thing with fear, but now I just channel it into a positive direction just like I do with worrying. Reframing your anxiety as excitement really works. It is as simple as it is powerful.

But here's the catch about telling yourself "I'm excited:" it doesn't actually lower the feelings surging through your body. It just gives your mind an explanation that empowers you.

My challenge to you is to test it out and see how it works for you personally. You can take that ability to reframe your thoughts into the bedroom if sometimes fear or anxiety takes over.

"You are braver than you believe, stronger than you seem, and smarter than you think"
                                                          --A. A. Milne

Consistently, when I ask women what they think they need in order to feel sexually empowered, without reservation, the number one answer I get is, "I want more confidence." Insecurity isn't sexy. A huge part of my work is teaching women about building confidence. I even wrote about becoming "sexy confident" in my previous book, *"MindStrength for Women"*.

My husband, Trent, came up with this term "sexy confidence" a few years ago and shared this with me. He said, *"The more and more confident you've become, the sexier you are to me. It's not just the changes in your body, but the changes in you and how you carry yourself. Your confidence is so attractive and makes me want to be even closer to you, to open up to you and connect with you in any way. You're sexy confident."*

So, why do most women seem to lack this 'sexy confidence'? Why is this crucial element of sexual currency hard to develop and hang on to?

Most of us have some work to do in this area. It's very hard to create the relationship, emotional connection, and sex of your dreams from a place of insecurity. You might be feeling emotionally disconnected, sexually frustrated, unable to have orgasms, feeling like you don't get as much from sex as your spouse does, or unable to ask for what you need sexually. Some people who are powerful in other areas of their lives (particularly women) sometimes lack the ability to get their needs met in the bedroom and often feel really small and dissatisfied there.

Remember, confidence is something you practice and gain. It's like a muscle. People aren't just born with confidence. Just like a muscle, that means you can learn to have more of it. We don't all operate with the same brand of confidence though. We have varying strengths and vulnerabilities.

It's essential to build on your unique strengths as you develop your sexy confidence.

Here are some strategies that worked for me to build true, lasting self-confidence--in and out of the bedroom.

WHAT CHANGED MY PERCEPTION

1. DO SOME RESEARCH

Sexual ignorance contributes greatly to people's lack of self-assurance. How do you build confidence in anything? In large part, by learning about it and getting good at it. That happens through practice.

When you develop skills to do something well, your confidence grows. So, you've got to find some version of adult sex education that's right for you, and work on the skills you want. Maybe you need to learn more about touch, flirtation, communication, or asking for what you want. Maybe you need to learn more about your body and how to have mind-blowing orgasms. Whatever it is you need to learn, it's a process almost completely controlled by you. That's great news.

Text the word **RESOURCES** to **801-505-9750**, for a list of my suggested book recommendations.

2. UNDERSTANDING TRUE CONFIDENCE

I love to address the topic of confidence. I want you to reconsider this definition of confidence:

"Confidence is a decision. It's the decision to try. A willingness to try."
--Mel Robbins, Author of *The 5 Second Rule*

As we get more comfortable in our own skin with basic confidence, we continue to grow on a path of self-improvement and wanting more.

But I want to share with you three myths and three truths to confidence.

Three myths about confidence:

1. *"It's a personality trait."* Wrong. Confidence is not determined by personality.

2. *"It's fixed."* False. It can come and go. What happens when you lose a race?

3. *"Confidence starts with belief."* Don't buy into this. It's not just about thinking positive. One of the biggest mistakes you can be thinking is that confidence begins with belief. That's what the personal development world may tell you, but it makes it almost impossible to stay positive long enough to gain confidence.

Three truths to confidence:

1. *Confidence is a skill.* I can do things to build it and grow it just like a muscle.

2. *Confidence is situational.* There will be areas of your life where you will have to work really hard at it, whereas in some areas of your life, it seems to come easy.

3. *Confidence begins with action.* If it begins with action, *you* have control over it. If you take little actions daily or weekly, you can grow more confidence as you see yourself progress.

3. EMBRACE BECOMING SEXY CONFIDENT

I believe that when your mind, body and spirit are aligned in working towards your purpose, you embody "sexy confidence." Sexy confident also means being informed, feeling empowered, and standing in your power while helping others do the same.

In the past, when I would hear the word "sexy," I would react in a negative way because of the meaning I had given that word. It was a dirty word to me. If my husband told me I was sexy, I would immediately feel naughty and dirty.

Recently I began to understand that the definition of "sexy" isn't just about sex or your body. "Sexy" is not just having beautiful lips, a perfect face, nice hair, or a nice body. Sexy goes beyond that. To me, "sexy" is the confident energy a person produces that attracts others. "Sexy" is the comfortable feeling of being who you are. It's about a person who embodies connection, attraction and growth.

When you have sexy confidence, people who meet you admire your sense of self-esteem and feel attracted to you. Not necessarily in a sexual way, but a curious way. When you walk into a room, people notice you because you hold your head up high and stand up tall. Not because of pride, but because you are confident and not concerned with what others might think about you or if they are judging you. You don't dwell on doubt, judgement from others, or uncertainty long enough to get you down. *That* is truly "sexy".

I want to have Trent jump in here and share more about how he and men he has talked with on this subject view sexy confidence and how it affects them in a relationship.

"First of all, you should know that Sarah becoming sexy confident was the catalyst to saving our marriage and creating a much deeper connection and bond between us.

We were going through a really hard time in our marriage and Sarah was about done with me. Probably because we didn't communicate and didn't understand each other. It was during this time that Sarah decided to focus on herself. Not in a selfish way, but in a good way. She made sure she worked out and ate healthy, not for me or to be more attractive, but simply because she wanted to feel good and have more energy.

Next, she started reading books, something she hardly did during our first 12 of marriage. Her daily habits started to change as she began to meditate daily and focus on what she was grateful for. Sarah also worked towards several other little goals that made her feel successful. The culmination of all this was when she started working with a coach to help her through some of the stuff in her head that was holding her back. The old beliefs and stories about who she was and what she was capable of that had been holding her back were starting to shift and disappear.

All of these things on their own might have seemed small and insignificant, but let me tell you what I saw. I saw a woman who was starting to discover what she wanted. She was passionate about things and worked hard to do them. She was creating the life and attitude that she wanted. She was someone I wanted to be more like and wanted to be closer to. Other people who she associated with also wanted to be around her more. Women noticed her newfound confidence. Men noticed too. I definitely noticed and started to feel like, "I better do something so I can keep up with her growth".

One of the things that we now realize was missing in our marriage up until then was: 1. I had business and personal goals that I was actively working toward, but Sarah had been feeling somewhat stuck "just being a mom" (even though that is one of the most important and impactful roles a person can have, she felt lost in it). 2. With one of us progressing and one feeling stuck, the passion in our marriage suffered.

Once Sarah started shifting, growing, and chasing her dreams, I started to want to be closer to her. I wanted to open up to her more and connect with her as she appeared almost as this new, sexy, confident woman that I hadn't known before.

To summarize, most men are attracted to confident women. No, not those who are simply faking confidence--we can usually see through that and recognize their insecurity. We are attracted to those who have put in the work to grow in different areas of their life and earn their confidence. When you are growing in one or more areas of your life, your confidence grows, and in healthy relationships, this usually makes a woman more 'sexy confident' in the eyes of her spouse. Just think about your own perspective for a moment. Do you want to be around confident (not cocky), fulfilled, successful people or insecure, unfulfilled, and struggling people?"

We all want to surround ourselves with success and confidence. You can create that pull in your own life as you work on becoming more confident in more and more areas of your life. People will notice and your spouse will notice. Hopefully they'll see that as a sign to also work on themselves and grow and not become jealous and/or insecure.

CHAPTER SEVEN

BUT MY BODY ISN'T WHERE I WANT IT TO BE

Just by virtue of being a woman in our culture, there's a good chance that some amount of body dislike is part of your reality. And disliking your body will interfere with your sexual comfort and satisfaction. Research has found that the worse a woman's body image is, the more likely she is to avoid sexual situations, and, when in them, the more likely that she will be more hesitant to tell a spouse what she wants. On the positive side, research has found that the more a woman likes her body, the more she initiates sex, the more sex she has, and the more orgasms she enjoys.

How much a woman dislikes her body and how much this interferes with her sex life is more about her body perceptions than about her actual body size and shape. I've talked with women who have the type of body our culture worships who feel too self-conscious to enjoy sex. I've also talked with women who have the type of body our culture ostracizes who are comfortable with their bodies during sex. Letting yourself relax during sex isn't about how much you weigh; it's about your feelings and thoughts about your body. And negative body thoughts are usually quite conscious.

As mentioned in Chapter Four, I introduced Brené Brown, "the shame researcher." She hosted a discussion between men and women about women believing that for a woman to be sexy, she couldn't have any "back fat". In her book, *Daring Greatly*, Brené Brown shared a response from one of the men,

"It's not about the back fat! You're worried about it, we are not. Stop making up all this stuff about what [men] are thinking. What we're really thinking is, do you love me? Do you care about me? Do you want me? Am I important to you? Am I good enough?

When it comes to sex, it feels like our life is on the line, and you're worried about that crap? When you want to be with us in that way, it makes us feel more worthy. We stand a little taller and believe in ourselves more."

I teach and empathize with women how important it is that we stop the self-sabotaging and we stop shaming our bodies. Men want connection, not just your body for pleasure.

We can gain "sexy confidence" and remain present when we are intimate, no matter what our bodies look like at the moment. Now you can see that it works for men's confidence too.

Sex is so much deeper for men than we realize. They are deeply hurt when they are rejected. Have you ever really considered how deeply this affects your man?

If you haven't had a conversation about this with him, please do. Ask him if he feels rejected because you care too much about yourself and your body image.

Aside from cases where health does not permit it, what's holding you back from enjoying sex in the body you have?

The simple answer is: *you.*

When I look back, my lack of communication and fear of authenticity were because of two things:

1. I didn't love myself.

2. I feared that Trent might not love me if he knew I wasn't perfect.

It's such a ridiculous thought to me now, but it kept me stuck for years!

Because I didn't love myself, I couldn't let others make the mistake of fully loving me either. I pushed people away from me; even Trent, who wanted to be close to me and love me and all of my imperfections. I wanted to stay hidden from others because I just couldn't push myself to the next level on the measuring stick of perfection. I chased perfection so much that it led me down a path of not loving myself.

I wrote about this in my first book. I shared the journey I went on to find my confidence, to create what Trent refers to as "sexy confidence." This again is the level of confidence that, when women have it, their man sees them as sexy, even when they are in their frumpy, around the house clothes, after spending the day cleaning or chasing around children. The sexy that comes through all the imperfections, back fat and all.

When a woman loves herself and has this self-confidence, her man can see that, and he wants more of her! That confidence makes you "sexy confident" to your man. He wants you, no matter what flaws you think you have.

The reason why I am painting this picture for you about my past is that I hope that I have captivated you enough to look into your own childhood and those experiences which shaped who you are today.

We may see that life has been blissful and calm. Others may see unhappiness and disconnection. Some may see anger and hatred from these experiences. However, whatever our situation was in the past, there is a way to see yourself blossom into the woman you are meant to be.

> *"Men learn to love women they are attracted to; women learn to be attracted to the men they love."*
>
> --Oscar Wilde, Poet

WHAT CHANGED MY PERCEPTION

1. THE HUMAN BODY IS MADE IN SUCH A WAY THAT TO GAIN STRENGTH IT HAS TO BE BROKEN FIRST

This may be a hard season you're walking through in your body. It will make you so much stronger, but only if you keep moving forward. The human body is filled with muscles that must be broken before they can grow strength. This season will not break you--it will grow you into who you need to be to have the amazing connection you want to have.

2. THERE IS A FINE LINE BETWEEN INSPIRATION AND JEALOUSY AND IT'S ONE I'VE WALKED MANY TIMES

I have carefully curated my life online and offline--to include people I find inspirational, people I look up to, people who excel in their field. They're motivating! Their success and messages help keep me focused, optimistic, and encourage me to continue to work hard.

But sometimes, I look at those exact same people and find myself not feeling good enough. I feel jealous, bitter, and defeated. I don't have time for that! (I'm guessing you don't either).

Thankfully, my years of experience with jealousy have given me some insight into what helps me stay on the "inspiration" side of the line.

1. Brené Brown says, "people are hard to hate up close." If I'm feeling jealous of someone I know in real life, I (try to) befriend them. It almost never fails; when I get to know people on a personal level, I often realize that we have a lot more in common than not.

2. Acknowledge that it might be an insight into something I really desire for myself. If it is, is it something I can take action on achieving? Do they have any advice for me? What can I learn from them?

3. Finally, I've noticed that jealousy is a hungry emotion. It needs to be fed with information. (which may explain why when I feel jealous of someone, I can't take my eyes off them). When this is the case, I've found distance helps. Unfollow, give yourself a break and give your mind a rest. You can always come back.

If you're like me, logically you know that the success of others does not diminish your accomplishments, but emotionally working through these emotions can be a bit more complex. But please remember, I don't have to compete, and neither do you. There is plenty of success, love, money, and talent to go around.

3. DON'T COMPARE YOURSELF TO ANYONE BUT YOU

As much as I discourage people from comparing themselves to others, we are naturally inclined to make comparisons as a means of learning about ourselves. It's not until you go to someone else's house that you realize that yelling all the time isn't necessarily normal. It's not until you see that drawing or singing doesn't come naturally to everyone else that you realize you have a gift.

We only judge people when they display a quality we could not accept in ourselves. We do this because we are beating ourselves up inside because we haven't quite figured out how to emulate that quality we see in them.

Every time I saw something or someone I judged or compared, I started saying to myself, "I am like that; they are within me." Own that aspect of yourself so you can unplug from others who have it.

Ram Dass taught a "Just Like Me" meditation. My dear friend, Jen Marco, shared it with me years ago and I use it often when I find that I am comparing myself to or judging others:

Just like me, he/she is seeking happiness.

Just like me, he/she is trying to avoid suffering in his/her life.

Just like me, he/she has known sadness, loneliness and despair.

Just like me, he/she is seeking to fulfill his/her needs.

Just like me, he/she is learning about life.

4. REALIZE MASS MEDIA IS DESIGNED TO MAKE YOU SEXUALLY INSECURE

With sex, there is no reality-based comparison for how you have sex. Porn is not real. Reality TV isn't real. Soap operas aren't real. The questions in many magazines can be trite. So, there's always a question mark about how you're "doing sex," and whether it's right. This leads to perpetual insecurity in nearly everyone about one of life's most important things.

When you do compare yourself, it's bound to be an unattainable ideal if it's based on mainstream media.

We can't all be Tim McGraw, Channing Tatum, Scarlett Johansson, Jennifer Lopez, or whomever the sexy flavor of the moment is. Our imaginations run wild about how sexually superior sexy stars must be because the camera is designed to make them look good at sex and seduction, even if they are totally awkward in real life. They always have the perfect line, perfect outfit, perfect body, or perfect flirty comeback. Add all the products you think you need in order to be desirable, and it's a constant uphill battle.

5. SELF-ACCEPTANCE IS SOMETHING YOU HAVE TO PRACTICE EVERY DAY

I needed to move through phases like self-hate, self-awareness, and neutrality before I found acceptance. Making peace with some parts of my body came way easier than others. But I know you are looking for some actionable tasks, so here you go:

1. Curate your life--both online and offline--so it supports how you wanna feel. Take inventory and cut out anything that doesn't support your goals.

2. Explore your shame. Brace yourself because this crap is uncomfortable, but self-acceptance is about embracing the totality of you--both delightful and difficult parts.

3. Be patient with yourself. You'll have good days and bad days. Probably a lot of "meh" days in there, too, and it's gonna take a while.

Where did the feelings about your body come from? Where are you when you feel them? Where did you learn this?

6. LOVE YOURSELF FROM THE INSIDE OUT

I have shared this exercise in my previous book, *MindStrength for Women*, but it continues to be a great practice for me to do.

Spending a couple of minutes in front of the mirror, working on yourself, makes a big difference in your confidence and well-being. Give yourself the time each day to do this exercise either in the morning or at night--or both. Stand in a wonder woman pose while speaking. See yourself as if you were looking through the eyes of God vs. your own judgement.

"I love you _____(name). I love and approve of myself, just as I am now. I am imperfect and wired to struggle, but I am worthy of love and belonging.

Step 1: What is awesome about you right now?

Step 2: I am _____

Step 3: Express gratitude for yourself

I am a child of God. I am a person of great value because God made me. I am an honorable person who is truly grateful for the opportunity life has given me. These are the qualities of the winner I was born to be.

Today is the first day of the rest of my life, and it is wonderful."

7. LINGERIE IS FOR YOU NOT HIM

How do you go from crazy daytime life to intimate wife? I've heard every excuse why women don't wear lingerie:

"What's the point? It's going to end up on the floor in a minute anyway."

"I don't like my boobs."

"I have bad tan lines."

"Gravity is not my friend."

We have all thought something like that, right? There is a common misconception that lingerie is for him. *It's not.* That's a perk, but lingerie is for *you*. It makes *you* feel sexy. It makes *you* feel more confident. I heard from a friend that lingerie takes you out of your everyday, mommy, housewife mode into sexy vixen mode, and no matter how practical your man is, he loves a sexy vixen!

Yes, you may focus on your stretch marks, your saggy skin, your tiny legs or big butt. However, he loves you the way you currently are, even if you don't feel sexy enough. Put on a piece of lingerie and cover the areas you don't quite enjoy but flaunt the other areas you do love about your body!

Movement creates emotion. The more you move in a piece of lingerie, the more you will begin to feel emotion within your body. Wear the lingerie piece as long as you need to feel confident and sexy in it. I've worn it while brushing my teeth, folding laundry in my bedroom, reading a book, dancing to music, wearing it under my clothing on a date (yes I do, give that a try), just to get used to wearing it. Once your body is in that state of arousal and you're ready to move forward with connecting, then you can give him permission to take it off you.

He already knows what you look like naked. When you show up in one of these, he will know where it's headed, and it is not to church!

If lingerie isn't currently a priority, I'm going to ask that you make it one. It's part of learning self-love if you don't currently feel so.

8. SEXY IS NOT A SIZE, IT'S AN ATTITUDE

Your attitude is everything in regard to confidence. To continue with this idea of clothing, I want you to imagine just for a moment a 3-year-old little girl in a princess dress. (I see my sweet Lynden, my daughter). Do you see her in your mind's eye? She begins twirling around and strutting her stuff around the room and radiating with confidence, right? As a grown woman, why can't we do that with lingerie, just like that little girl? The more you begin to feel comfortable in that space, the more it can carry outside the bedroom into other areas of your life.

One of my favorite movies on this topic of confidence is *I Feel Pretty,* and I'd like to quote the closing speech where Amy Schumer is on stage and speaks out:

"When we were little girls, we had all the confidence in the world. We let our belly hang out and dance and play. Then things happen to make us question ourselves.

You grow up and doubt yourself over and over again until you lose all that confidence, self-esteem, and faith that you started with.

But what if we didn't want those moments to be gone? What if we were stronger than that? What if we didn't care about how we look or how we sounded? What if we never lost that little girl confidence? So, this is me, and I'm proud to be me!"

9. MY WORTH IS SET WITH GOD AND EVERYTHING ELSE IS AN EXPERIENCE

A friend of mine, Amy, shared something her therapist taught her. It's a beautiful statement that has a profound impact just by speaking it out loud. Your body and your worth with God are set already. You don't need to work for your worth. Show up, unapologetically be you, because God made you the way you are. Everything else is just an added bonus of the experiences you get to have here on this earth. Hanging on to negative thoughts about yourself is like letting them live rent-free in your head. They don't belong there because God didn't put them there.

CHAPTER EIGHT

THE FEMALE SEXUAL RESPONSE CYCLE

When I get in front of women, the first question I ask is if they've ever heard of "The Female Sexual Response Cycle." About 80% of them have not. Knowing the lack of understanding about this cycle motivates me to better educate women and men on its existence. Understanding this cycle transformed my marriage, and I know it will do the same for yours.

Have you ever been curious as to what exactly happens to your body *before, during, and after* sex?

Women generally have a significant learning curve to understanding how their body works when it comes to sex, whereas men have had a head start on their sexual awareness due to the external nature of their sexual organs and generally more curious nature.

Learning and understanding the phases of the female sexual response cycle will help you identify what phase or phases you may be struggling with. The female sexual response cycle describes the physical and emotional changes that women go through as they become sexually aroused.

Keep in mind that there are a number of different sexual response cycle models used by sex therapists and researchers, so this is only one example that I personally love to teach and makes more sense to me.

I learned five phases of the female sexual response from sex therapist Laura Brotherson's book, *And They Were Not Ashamed.* She explains beautifully what this cycle is in 5 steps:

1. Warm-up

2. Foreplay / Arousal

3. Desire

4. Orgasm / Climax

5. Afterglow

"How a person experiences sexual response is unique to them. It's normal for people to spend more time in one phase than another, experience the phases in different sequences, and/or not to experience all of the phases during a sexual experience. For example, not everyone will experience an orgasm every time they engage in sexual activity.

Going through each of the phases during a sexual experience are not necessary to have a pleasurable sexual experience. Many people have very satisfying experiences without having an orgasm."

--Laura Brotherson, LMFT, CST, CFLE

WARM-UP

It is understandable that the warm-up phase is often overlooked or ignored, especially by men. But for women, we see sex as more of a decision. We want to feel comfortable and safe before any clothing comes off us. As a woman, this is a key part of our sexual experience. The warm-up happens outside of the bedroom. The warm-up is non-sexual, and this where we emotionally connect at the beginning of this cycle.

As women, our brain is constantly thinking about the next thing to do or what hasn't been done, and/or what we want to happen, etc. We've got a long list going on in our brains. We need to brain dump whatever is on our minds, to get it out in the open air and talk, talk, talk until we've let our spouse know our list of things on our minds.

For women, we may need some help from the men in regard to household duties to free up some time from the lists in our minds. Or it could be to solve a parenting problem. However, the man's willingness to be a partner in the household responsibility must be constant and genuine to be effective.

I've personally found that for me when Trent is an active participant in the household responsibilities, for example by doing the dishes, I am aware that he is showing me he loves me by doing that act of service. Acts of service is my primary love language. I'll share more on love languages in the following chapter, Chapter Nine.

As men learn to view their active interest and participation in the home and family as an integral part of their wife's ability to engage sexually, both spouses' needs will be better fulfilled. This assistance can ease a wife's load and free her up to relax and engage in some of the warm-up.

Another aspect to this part of the cycle is the attention to personal hygiene for both of you. You can do this by having smooth skin, brushing your teeth, and smelling nice. You've got to be aware of your senses in this part; allow yourself to tap into what is sensual about you, whether you are going to have sex or not.

In Chapter Nine, *"I can't be present in the moment,"* you will learn how this part of the cycle is critical to help you be more grounded and present with your husband during sex.

FOREPLAY / AROUSAL

Women are like water found in a stream in a forest: we are a source of life and nourishment the same way the stream feeds the nearby plants. Our actions take longer, as do our responses. We take a long time to warm up, but when we do, we can stay turned on for longer. But men are like fire. Men can burn through the forest quickly, get to orgasm, and then are extinguished almost immediately.

Foreplay is not a one-size-fits-all. It comes in as many varieties as there are individuals, and it can change with circumstances and moods. You are the best sexual teacher for your spouse. Only you can teach them what you want, and this part of the cycle is where you get to explore your own body. You are the authority of your body!

Women are empowered to create the mood rather than waiting for the mood. You can accomplish this by doing the three T's which Laura speaks of in her book: talk, touch, and time. This allows you to prepare yourself mentally and physically. The talk, touch, and time devoted to this phase provides the opportunity for you to get in the mood and be an active participant in lovemaking.

Movement creates emotion. In the warm-up phase, your survival needs are satisfied; now is the time to promote pleasure. Pleasure comes to us through any of our senses, and especially when savoring your spouse's touch.

It is through the senses where we first get "in touch." To be in touch is to know what we feel, to be awake and aware. To be in touch is to be connected. Through emotion, pleasure, and sensation, we enter the complex realm of sexuality. This is a place where we dissolve our boundaries and enter into intimacy with another.

Laura also shares that *"every person has erogenous areas on their body that when touched or stimulated increase sexual arousal. It is the opportunity and responsibility of husband and wife to embark on a lifelong treasure hunt to learn and develop each other's sexual hot spots."* You have up to 15 erogenous areas on your body. For example, some people may not realize that ears, necks, wrists, fingers, and elbows are common erogenous zones. Now go on a treasure hunt to find them!

What is pleasurable and what is a turnoff? As a couple, you must share what you find pleasurable and what is a turnoff. Let each other know. How will he know what you're feeling or what you want him to do if you don't tell him or show him? Women can also teach without words as they guide their husbands hands or moan their approval when they experience particularly pleasing caresses or activities.

"Foreplay is a vital aspect of any sexual relationship because it gives each partner the time their body needs to prepare physically for sexual activity. Without engaging in foreplay, a man may not give his body enough time to achieve and maintain a firm erection necessary for penetration."

--Laura Brotherson, LMFT, CST, CFLE

Foreplay is also incredibly important for women. A woman who does not engage in foreplay may not increase her arousal enough to prepare for comfortable sexual activities like intercourse. Our bodies aren't designed to just be thrown on the bed and penetrated without the proper time to be aroused. As a woman becomes excited, her vagina produces natural lubrication and expands to accommodate comfortable penetration.

Without these changes, intercourse may be uncomfortable, or even painful. Foreplay can play a crucial role in overcoming vaginal dryness and preventing discomfort or pain during intercourse. Women need to give themselves adequate time for vaginal expansion and natural lubrication. To give their bodies enough time to prepare for sex, it's suggested that women spend at least 10-15 minutes engaging in foreplay that they find sexually arousing. This can include receiving a body massage, engaging in dirty talk, or whatever else she needs to get sufficiently aroused.

For women and men experiencing arousal, nipples harden, breath quickens, the skin becomes flush, and blood flows to the genitals. This phase can last anywhere from a few minutes to several hours. Excitement or arousal is the combination of mind and body. Ask yourself, "am I feeling emotionally and/or physically excited?"

The amount of time spent during foreplay will vary from person to person and from situation to situation. For example, one spouse may be feeling stressed or struggling to become aroused, so they may need to spend more time in the foreplay period. The same couple may only need to engage in a few minutes of foreplay during their next sexual encounter. There is no such thing as too much foreplay as long as both spouses are enjoying themselves. Unfortunately, people can and often do engage in too little foreplay.

Foreplay is also necessary for men struggling with erectile difficulties. As a man becomes aroused, blood flows to his genitals, allowing him to achieve an erection. For men experiencing erectile difficulties, the blood flow necessary for an erection is impeded, by physical and/or mental factors, making it difficult for men to get or keep an erection and making intercourse difficult or impossible. Taking the time to increase his excitement can help raise the likelihood that he will be able to achieve and maintain an erection.

Foreplay happens after the last orgasm! As couples, we should be in foreplay often. Foreplay is an energy investment into each other.

Refer to Chapter Ten, *"I don't know what turns me on"* to get a better understanding about this phase.

DESIRE

Desire is the yearning, want, or interest in initiating or responding to sexual advances. Desire is commonly identified as the first phase in the human sexual response. Common sense tells us that's so.

But I've found that, although I might not have been thinking sexual thoughts or feeling particularly sexy, I pushed myself to get started when my spouse approached me. This felt good, and I found myself getting into it. I thought I lacked sexual desire but have found that for me, desire doesn't happen until I have been physically aroused. Movement needs to happen to create that emotion, like you read about in the Foreplay/Arousal phase.

> *"So, for those of you who thought you weren't sexual, it may be that you have always been sexual, but just didn't understand that you needed sexual stimulation and arousal before sexual desire could occur."*
> --Laura Brotherson, LMFT, CST, CFLE

Sometimes I just need to go forward with the sexual experience, committing myself mentally to it.

Choosing it. I have to remind myself that I got into it last time, and I liked it. Once the stimulation is sufficient, I begin to love the experience. You'd think the need for a conscious choice would go away, but sex is still a decision I have to make *every* time. It's like an "act of faith" to embark on the sexual experience without sexual desire first in hand.

Your brain is your largest sex organ. It will either work in your favor or it won't, depending on what you tell it. Sex is a mind game and sex will test your mental strength. Train your brain to understand how to relax and allow it to become part of reaching an orgasm.

With that said, you may feel that you have a low desire for sex, and it's good for you to find out why. Below are some areas to look into as a cause for a low sex drive if this is something you are concerned with:

- Illness
- Medications
- Hormonal imbalance
- Sexual, physical or emotional abuse
- Depression
- Low self-esteem
- Poor body image
- Fatigue
- Stress
- Time constraints
- Going along to get along
- Lack of forgiveness

Many physical factors play a role in your desire. You have quite a bit of control over all these factors, which means that you can directly affect your sex life by optimizing your physical lifestyle. These are only a few things. We women are a mess sometimes, aren't we? We are just plain complicated.

Honestly, our desire is *primarily* affected by three components. If you struggle with one of these, then you aren't really feeling the spark to get on that bed and make love to him. The three components are:

1. A healthy attitude towards sex. If you know that you view your sexuality as unhealthy or something that you get irritated by and have a bad attitude about, then you're not going to have a desire for sex.

2. The ability to get your body in a state of arousal. You have trained your brain to shut off the idea of sex when you began to feel the sensations of your body being aroused by certain things. You would suppress that arousal and send a message to your brain, "not today!" Then it would shut it off.

3. Proper sexual functioning. I'm not a doctor, nor will I ever be one, so if the first two aren't something you struggle with, but you still don't have that desire, then you should seek professional help either from a doctor or

therapist to see what may be contributing to your lowered sex drive internally.

When we can come into our sexual response cycle knowing where we are stuck and acknowledging it, we can help promote its function again. We should then share that with our spouse and come up with solutions on how to create a different experience when it comes to our desire.

I am only barely scraping the surface on this topic of desire. But the key here is to *want* sex, so be sure to read Chapter Eleven, *"I never want it...is that normal?"* and Chapter Twelve *"Why does my spouse want it so much more than me?"* It will help you troubleshoot your shortcomings with desire.

ORGASM

Some women regard orgasm as unnecessary because of their difficulty or inability to experience it, or because of the skill, time, and effort it may require. But God created women with the capacity not only for orgasmic expression, but also the capacity to experience multiple orgasms.

I like the way Dr. Marie Robinson describes orgasm in her book, *The Power of Sexual Surrender*:

"Orgasm is the physiological response which brings sexual intercourse to its natural and beautiful termination...in the moment just preceding orgasm, muscular tension suddenly

arises. At the moment of greatest muscular tension all sensations seem to take one further rise upward. The woman tenses beyond the point where, it seems, it would be possible to maintain such tension for a moment longer. And indeed, it is impossible, and now her whole body suddenly plunges into a series of muscular spasms. These muscular spasms take place within the vagina itself, shaking the body with waves of pleasure. If a woman is sexually satisfied by her orgasmic experience, she will discharge the neurological and muscular tension developed in the sexual build-up."

Sometimes a woman does not know if she has experienced an orgasm. If you feel your vagina contracting involuntarily, starting with a feeling of excitement before transitioning into feeling calm and physically satisfied, you can take this as evidence that you have had an orgasm, though perhaps a weak one.

Orgasm might also be described as pleasurable sensations that slowly build until the sexual tension bursts into a shooting star throughout the body.

Laura Brotherson in her book, *And They Were Not Ashamed,* shares about orgasms, *"the important question for many couples is not so much what an orgasm is, but how to create it. Lovemaking is an art that requires knowledge, practice and skillful application of what is pleasurable and sexually arousing. In the same way that a musician can become more knowledgeable and skillful, a couple can learn to freely and frequently experience the ecstasy of orgasm."*

Did you know that as a woman you can experience five types of orgasms?

1. Clitoral--*"95% of women require clitoral stimulation to climax"* says Laura Mintz, Ph.D. and author of *Becoming Cliterate*. It can be easily reached; you can have a clitoral orgasm with your clothes on.

2. Vaginal--The first 1-3 inches inside your vagina is packed with nerve endings and is stimulated by the in-and-out motion of intercourse. This orgasm is a little deeper and longer lasting. On average, it can take up to 14-18 min to get aroused as a woman. Once fully aroused, vaginal tenting occurs, expanding the vagina up to 6 inches, making penetration more comfortable.

3. G-spot--The G-spot is a highly erogenous area on the front of the vaginal wall of the urethral sponge that can be stimulated during sexual activity. It is the female equivalent to the prostate. When stimulated, you will feel the same sensation as you would feel when you feel the need to pee. In order to have the

orgasm happen, you need to get over this sensation and just let it go!

4. Nipple--When the nipples are stimulated, oxytocin is released, which causes the same uterine and vaginal contractions associated with orgasm. Not everyone can experience this type of orgasm.

5. Anal--There are shared nerves from the anterior wall of the rectum to the vagina. So it may be possible for sexual arousal to occur from rectal stimulation. Plus, the legs of the clitoris stretch all the way back to the anus, so backdoor stimulation can fire up the clitoris, too.

I'll expand more about orgasm in Chapter Thirteen, *"I feel like I'm broken."*

While you can have a great, connected sexual experience without orgasm, it is something most humans want to experience. The goal when having sex is not orgasm. It is to connect your bodies and experience love and pleasure. Orgasm is a beautiful, amazing consequence that can come from sex, but you are okay if you haven't experienced an orgasm.

When you remove the pressure to perform and to achieve orgasm, you will enjoy sex more. You may even find yourself experiencing the unexpected. Allow time, communication, and the education in this book to help you progress in feeling more relaxed and more open to receive pleasure.

In a study by Kim Wallen, Ph.D. and Elisabeth A. Lloyd, Ph.D. on female sexual arousal they found if you are one of the 10% of women who has never had an orgasm, there may still be hope. Even if you've been married 40+ years and never experienced an orgasm, you are okay. My day is always made brighter when I hear things like I heard from a woman in her sixties who I recently worked with.

"You'll never believe what happened!" she told me. *"After 40 years of marriage, I finally know what an orgasm feels like! When you taught me how powerful it is when we direct our thoughts and brain to focus on the sensation in our clitoris and drop the expectations to perform, things changed for me. I tried what you taught along with the cream you recommended; it was like handing Dumbo a magic feather and now I can fly!"*

AFTERGLOW

This part of the cycle was a game changer for our marriage! Afterglow is about emotionally connecting after you've just felt sexual satisfaction followed by a state of utter calm. The body feels absolutely quiet. This is the part when maybe your man rolls over and falls asleep, right? Wake him up!

Emotional connection not only happens during the first phase of Warm-up, but it also happens at the end in Afterglow. Teach him this part. He needs to remain attentive and loving throughout the afterglow, sharing this moment of closeness with you, his wife.

Laura Brotherson also shares in her book, *And They Were Not Ashamed,* that *"you are emotionally, spiritually and physically content--even if it's only for a few moments. There is no timetable on this but it's an experience where you recommitment your love and trust, reuniting you as a couple in the most sacred and spiritual experiences God created within the covenant of marriage."*

In the past, before understanding the importance of this last step, I just wanted to clean up and move on with my day/night once we finished having sex. But now Trent and I have found that we are able to talk to each other more about sex to find what works and what doesn't during this Afterglow phase. This lets us create more pleasure and a better connection during intimacy. We now feel like our needs are being met and can confidently express what we want during this intimate time together.

A great option is to find a list of questions you can begin to ask each other about your views on sex.

A great resource for these types of questions is a book written by John and Julie Gottman, Ph.D., titled *Eight Dates.* Refer to their chapter about sex and intimacy. They also have a relationship app that is a great resource called *Gottman Card Decks.* Check out the section, *"Sex Questions to Ask a Man or*

Woman." It has some great questions to get the ball rolling and get the two of you communicating about this subject.

Please refer to Chapter Fourteen, *"I don't know enough about sex, so I won't talk about it"* to get more ideas in regard to this phase in the cycle.

CHAPTER NINE

I CAN'T BE PRESENT IN THE MOMENT

Many men and women struggle with staying present during sex. You may find your mind wandering at times, going to the last TV show you were watching, or to-do lists, project deadlines, shopping checklists. You may find yourself worrying about some upcoming event, or reliving a past one.

These are common distractions that don't allow us to be present and enjoy the act of sex. There are other types of thought as well that also inhibit our ability to fully enjoy sex.

You might worry about whether you are doing it right. Are you making the right noises? Should you be doing something differently? Does my body look good in this lighting?

These types of thoughts (when you start evaluating your performance) are what the author, Emily Nagoski of *Come as You Are,* shares about the concept of "spectatoring."

"Spectatoring is the art of worrying about sex while you're having it. Rather than paying attention to the pleasant and tingly things your body is experiencing, it's like you're floating above the bed watching, noticing how your breasts fall or the squish of cottage cheese on the back of your thigh or the roll at your belly, or you're worried about the sex you're having instead of enjoying the sex you're having."

And worry is the opposite of arousal. It is the anti-arousal, because anxiety slams on the brakes. Turning off anxiety eases off the brakes, letting your sexual response flow smoothly forward. We know the phrase "performance anxiety" because men experience a similar phenomenon, worrying about whether they'll be able to get and sustain an erection – which, in turn, makes it more difficult for them to get erections. Women, whose erections are non-obvious and unnecessary, strictly speaking, for intercourse, haven't been given credit for this particular problem, but it affects us too, often in the form of spectatoring.

Studies have shown that when you start spectatoring, both your sexual performance and enjoyment decrease. Not really surprising, is it?

It's hard to enjoy something you aren't focusing on, and it's hard to be good at something you're not really paying attention to.

These types of thoughts are a distraction. They take you away from enjoying what's happening at that moment. You are "in your head" and thinking, analyzing, or worrying too much.

When women are up in their heads too much, estrogen makes it so that we are looking for danger, looking to see if we are safe, wondering what we are missing. On the other hand, testosterone says, "I wanna have sex, now!"

Regardless of which type of thoughts creep into your mind, they usually lead to some negative thoughts about yourself like:

• *I should have done that yesterday.*

• *How do we always run out? I should know to buy more toilet paper by now.*

• *Work is going to be such a drag tomorrow. I can't stand Bob's meetings.*

• *I'm such a bad mom.*

• *My sister is probably mad at me. I let her down when I didn't show up for lunch.*

• *I should be a better lover, in better shape, or what-have-you.*

If you look at how our brains work, it is no surprise that our minds wander. Your brain is designed to problem solve, and in the absence of a problem, your brain will come up with one to solve. Unfortunately, often the problem it wants to create so that it can solve something is, "I should be better than I am."

When you are in your head like this during sex, it doesn't mean you don't love your spouse, or that you aren't attracted to them. It doesn't mean you aren't enjoying sex, or that you aren't interested in sex. It just means you're normal.

The good news is that even though these wandering thoughts happen to many people during sex, and all people at some time or another during other parts of regular life, you can do something about it. Though it may take a lifetime to perfect, you should see improvements fairly quickly with a bit of practice.

I will share what worked for me in staying more focused and present during sex.

WHAT CHANGED MY PERCEPTION

1. BRAIN DUMP

A brain dump is how I get out of my head--or get my head out of everything else.

When your brain is fried, it's because there's way too much going on in there. There's a fancy psychological term "cognitive load," which basically means your brain can only handle so much. If there's too much going on, your mind will start to spill over, like filling a glass with water until it is full, and continuing to add more water. Next thing you know, it's all over the place. You're left with this big mess to clean up.

But I digress. You need to do a cognitive *unload* before your brain spills over.

Take out a piece of paper (or a few!), or better yet, share these with your spouse. Dump out everything that's on your mind. What are you worried about? What do you have to get done? When will you make those photo albums you said you'd design online from last year's trip? What am I going to wear tomorrow? Whatever you need to get out that's weighing on your mind, write or speak it out loud.

Take that time to clear your mind and close any open loops. Take 10 minutes and think about anything you have left undone. It helps your brain to be okay with releasing those things once you know that your mind doesn't have to keep reminding you about these things. Now you have them on a written list or have spoken them to someone who might help you remember some of the things on your mind.

2. EXPECT DISTRACTIONS, EVEN THOSE DARN KIDS

Distractions happen to everyone. Our minds all wander from time to time, even when we want to be present, like during sex. About the worst thing you can do is get upset or worried about it. Then you become worried about the distraction, which is more distracting!

Instead, just accept that this is normal; it happens. Acknowledge the thought, and let it go. Even if you have to ignore those kids pounding on the door (probably the hardest distraction for any mom to choose to ignore). I'm still working on this one from time to time.

3. KNOW AND UNDERSTAND YOUR SPOUSE'S LOVE LANGUAGE

People feel and express love differently and understanding your spouse's love language is key to a long-lasting relationship. Different people perceive love in different ways and use different words and actions to express the 5 love languages that Dr. Gary Chapman describes in his book, *The 5 Love Languages*.

1. Positive, uplifting **words of affirmation** are a powerful way to express love. Give verbal compliments. This is most effective when done in a simple and straightforward manner.

2. Spend **quality time** with your spouse. Undivided attention. It's not enough to simply be together in the same room. Quality time is about focusing on your spouse and nothing else, even if loads of distractions lurk behind every corner. Furthermore, spending quality time with your

spouse is a primary way for both of you to feel loved, respected, and appreciated.

3. **Gifts** are visual symbols of love, and surprising your spouse with regular presents, regardless of their monetary value, is a great way to show affection. The value lies in the whole process– from having the idea to give a gift, to going out to get or make it and, finally, the gesture of presenting this symbol of love to your spouse.

4. Doing useful things for your spouse is a common way to express love. These **acts of service** are essentially things you know your spouse would appreciate you handling–things like vacuuming or paying the bills, for example, or maybe grocery shopping, helping the kids with their schoolwork, or taking the dog to the vet. To be truly legitimate, such acts need to be voluntary. So, instead of asking what your spouse can do for you, ask what you can do for your spouse.

5. **Physical touch** is a powerful way to show your love. You can try touching him or her in unexplored places and asking for feedback about what's pleasurable. Work hard at understanding which subtler forms of physical contact can fill your spouse's love tank. Vary the pressure of touch.

Go take the free test to find out your love language and invite your spouse to also: 5lovelanguages.com.

To take this language to another level and ease, Dr. Gary Chapman created an app for couples called *The Love Nudge*. *Love Nudge for Couples* will help you put concepts of *The 5 Love Languages* into action in ways that are easy, obvious, and satisfying. It's like a fitness app for relationships.

Trent and I have been using it, and I am grateful to have this tool to help me be more intentional about how I express my love to Trent. It gives you reminders and gentle nudges to remember your love goals. I'm sure you will find it a great resource, too.

4. MINDFUL SEX

Mindful sex is when you're totally and completely immersed in the physical sensations of your body.

Practice staying focused in regular daily life. Sex isn't the only time that we aren't present in our lives. We often get distracted by cell phones, social media, stray thoughts, to-do lists, etc. It can happen when you are out with friends, with family, at church during sermons (I can't be the only one), in work meetings, or while driving.

Be conscious of when you are distracted, then make a choice to get out of the past (analyzing choices and events) and out of the future (planning or thinking about how possible scenarios in daily life might play out) and instead focus on the present moment. The more you consciously do this, the faster your brain will create new neural pathways and create new routines to pull you back to the present when you're distracted.

Turning your brain on during sex can be done through mindfulness, which is a simple but very potent remedy for a lot of psychological problems. Mindfulness increases happiness, decreases depression, diminishes anxiety, and even helps people deal with chronic illness and pain. Most important for our purposes: it leads to better sex and more orgasms.

In a nutshell, mindfulness is simply focusing completely on what's happening in the present moment. It means putting your mind and body in the same place. I'm sure you've been in a situation like this; your body is being touched by your spouse while your mind is thinking about an email you need to respond to. Yes?

Being mindful takes practice. I've had to develop a saying that reminds me to come back to the present. I say to myself "*bed not head*" to move myself back to the moment whenever distracting thoughts come in. Still, most mindfulness teachers recommend that when a distracting thought occurs, simply notice it. Don't get stuck on it and don't judge it. Don't try to force it to go away, either. In mindfulness, distracting thoughts are noticed and observed, then released without judgement. For me, it's helpful to visualize a gently moving conveyor belt that is taking that bothersome thought away.

Taking a really deep breath is also one of the most useful strategies to bring myself back to the present moment during sex. I then combine deep breathing with scent perception to help me to nuzzle into Trent's neck and breathe his scent. His pheromones is a signal to myself to get present again.

Mind-blowing sex means that your mind is not working; only your body is reacting. This is exactly what mindfulness helps you do. Having an orgasm requires letting go of control and not thinking at all. That's why studies have unequivocally shown that teaching women to be mindful leads them to be more sexually responsive and satisfied. Busy brains are not for the bedroom. So, start practicing mindfulness today. I love my *Headspace* app to help me practice. Go find something to kickstart you into this new world.

5. WOMEN NEED TO BE BROUGHT INTO FEELING SEXUAL

This is one where your husband gets to help you stay more present. When husbands and wives communicate about this transition and figure it out in their marriage, it is a game changer.

One thing I wish all husbands could understand is that your wife desires to feel sexy and be told and showed that you find her very attractive. She wants to be touched in non-sexual ways leading up to foreplay and sex. She wants to feel that you love her, not just want her for sex, but that you truly love and care for her, and you are there to protect her.

Guys, help her discover her sexuality by taking it *slow*. She needs foreplay, so pace yourself when warming her up, and give her honest, genuine compliments. Tell her what she does that drives you mad, or what it is about her that turns you on.

Slow. Down. Whatever speed you think is slow enough for her, make it twice as slow. This will draw out her sexuality as you honor and respect her speed of warm up and arousal. She will want you even more. Make her get to the point of almost begging you to have sex (yes, this is something we get to create in healthy sexual relationships).

Trent has learned from my feedback (ladies, your man won't know unless you tell him) that half speed of what he thinks my speed is, is closer to the speed that I want and need. He also learned that the best sex we've had is when he goes so slow during foreplay that even I feel it is slow and feel teased and want sex right then. I have no problem staying fully present until reaching climax when I feel wanted and desired. Then to add that I really enjoy when he is paying attention to my needs and my arousal/warm up speed. Tell your husband what draws out your sexual desire, and don't be afraid to share with him and guide him through that.

6. REFER TO STEP 1, WARM-UP, IN THE FEMALE SEXUAL RESPONSE CYCLE IN CHAPTER EIGHT

When your spouse recognizes how important it is for you, as the woman, to connect emotionally before sex happens, he will truly understand how to make you feel comfortable and safe to stay present in the moment together.

CHAPTER TEN

I DON'T KNOW WHAT TURNS ME ON

For years I felt nothing. I felt numb. I felt the opposite of sexy. It's like it didn't even register with me.

I got caught up feeling distracted and disconnected when it came to sexual pleasure and desire. I didn't identify any desire within myself and when Trent would come on to me, I found it difficult to even feel. How did I even get here in the first place?

"How do I feel in my body when my husband starts to touch me?"

I do remember that during the first two years of marriage, I would respond more positively to touch, but then became numb after I had our first baby. The demanding mom life set in, and I got distracted and stressed, and it took me away. I didn't want to be touched and didn't want or feel I deserved pleasure from sex. Whenever Trent would try and figure me out and ask, "what turns you on?" I honestly could not answer and didn't want to think about it.

In our culture, it is almost as if men have this "duty" to be good in bed and are expected to know how to turn you on. Women are expected to know what they want and communicate that with their spouse, but women often don't know what they want. Most of us have never learned from anyone that is any good at teaching about sex (parent, sibling, friend, girlfriends, etc), so we are left to figure it out on our own and expected to just be good at sex.

For many women, even bringing up the subject of sex makes them shut down. I sure did. Most of the time, this was because of my background and how I first learned--or didn't learn--about sex.

My parents never mentioned the word "sex," and I was too afraid to ask any questions, as I didn't feel it was okay to talk about. I created negative associations around sex and those feelings carried into my marriage for many years.

Women who were raised in an environment where sex was taboo or treated as shameful often have a hard time letting go of those negative associations with sex. This may sound obvious, but I can't tell you how many women, including me, treat their sexuality as a negative thing, hiding it from themselves or keeping it hidden from their spouses. They blocked from truly embracing their sexuality because they judge it as something bad, dirty, or morally wrong, and this makes it nearly impossible for these women to discover what they want and what turns them on.

In order to begin to discover what turns you on, so you can share that with your spouse, we have to first analyze and discard beliefs that are not true and that no longer serve you.

It has taken me a long time, but I am finally open to receive pleasure and have allowed myself to figure out what turns me on. I now see sex as the most powerful and intimate way to connect and express love and desire with my husband. Here are a few things that changed for me.

WHAT CHANGED MY PERCEPTION

1. I STARTED TO FIND OUT WHAT TURNS ME ON

"What turns you on?"

Trent asked me that question often and he was often frustrated that I couldn't figure that out and couldn't explain it to him either.

It really came down to not wanting to know. I didn't want to explore what turned me on for the longest time as I felt that would mean I want sex and am a *bad girl*.

Now, before you try to answer the question of what turns you on, keep in mind four things:

1. There is no right or wrong answer to this question.

2. There may be many answers to that question, and that is okay.

3. Your answer may change over time, depending on your mood, the time of the month, your age, or even who you are with.

4. You may not even know the answer to that question... yet. That's okay; there is not a deadline to figuring that out. Take your time.

I want to help as many women as possible to think about what experiences or narratives ignite their desire. What acts or touch by your spouse can be used to help warm you up? Some women are reading the *Twilight* books or romance novels, and they find that the story line allows them to connect to this important part of themselves and start to identify what turns them on. Their desire and understanding of what makes them feel wanted, desired, sexy, and turned on becomes easier to share. But reading novels doesn't do it for every woman.

One way to find out what turns you on is to try new things with your spouse. Ask questions and have conversations about what is safe for you, yet novel and new. Explore new touch and new foreplay options. Talk about your fantasy of having sex with him on the beach or about something else that feels a little outside of "missionary position sex."

Ask your spouse to change up how they approach initiating sex with you. Go through Chapter Eight, "*The Female Sexual Response Cycle*," and clarify, together, on what helps you move from each of the five stages. Talk about your sexual experiments afterwards and find out what you did or didn't like about the new things you tried.

When you come from a place of curiosity and reserve judgement until after you've both discussed your experience, it allows you to be less constrained to your typical sex routine. If you tried something and it didn't work for you, just be clear and honest. Your relationship is unique to you. Don't feel pressured to enjoy what you may have heard your friends or other women enjoy.

2. FIND VISUAL AND EMOTIONAL STIMULUS FOR WHAT TURNS YOU ON TO YOUR SPOUSE

For me, if Trent wears his hat backwards anytime, I pay more attention to him. I can't put into words why a hat does it for me, but it does something to my eye! Another visual is Trent dressed up in a sharp-looking, fitted suit. The suit must be fitted though. I realized this was a turn on for me when I went suit shopping with him two years ago in England. We went to a fancy suit shop where he was properly fitted for the first time in our marriage, and I knew right there that we were never going to buy him a cheap suit again. Oh boy--it's a huge turn on for me! I know it's a simple visual stimulus, but it works.

Can you think of something that he wears or does either visually or emotionally to draw your attention to him?

3. ASK FOR WHAT YOU WANT

This was hard for me at first. I had to learn to share with Trent what I wanted sexually. In order to do this, I had to open my mind to learn and open my body to explore what I enjoyed and what I didn't.

Talk about exposing yourself.

By being vulnerable in sharing what you want and what you don't will make for a pleasant experience. This vulnerability started with dropping the fear of exploring my body. I had to learn to recognize what felt good to me and give that feedback to Trent--even in the middle of having sex.

This instant feedback helped him and me both to learn what was good and what could be adjusted in the moment to make it better. Talking during sex is okay and makes sex better, quicker.

The more confident I became, the easier it was to ask for what I want. You may also find that this is a huge turn on for your man. Many men love a confident woman who clearly tells him how she wants him to pleasure her. Claim what you want, and get yourself in that vulnerable state to express it.

Can you describe in one sentence what you want?

> Asking directly for what you want without explanations is an expression of confidence. It's hard for most people to ask for what they want, and it requires you to have an intimate understanding with your own desire. This comes over time and with practice.

When you have that inner knowledge and familiarity with your true desire, it makes it much easier to ask for it and get it. Of course, when you are in a relationship with someone who is insecure and you confidently ask for what you really want, they might be intimidated into going along with your version of things because they don't know what else to ask for. It can be easy to miss each other altogether, create a poor power dynamic, or have needs go unmet.

Try to keep communication open on both sides and confidently ask him to share what he wants.

Sharing our wants is a skill we have in other parts of our life, like when it comes to food or shopping. We can share with our spouse, "Yes, I want sushi." "No, I don't like the color of that dress, but I'm open to trying on the red dress."

I was inspired to try this exercise that was shared by Kristin Hodson, *LCSW, CST* from her Instagram account (@kristinbhodson)

What you'll do is get two pieces of paper and write down these three words: want, will and won't, into three columns:

WANT	WILL	WON'T
ex. Tickling	ex. Wrestling or "play fighting"	ex. Fingers inside vagina
ex. Nipples sucked & licked	ex. Using a bedroom accessory	ex. Anal sex

Then, you and your spouse will start writing the things that pertain to these three words. The WANT column is a Yes! Yes you are wanting to try these ideas. The WILL column are things that you are willing to try that you haven't experienced yet. Then the last column of WON'T are things that are just hard to swallow and think about at this point.

Not only will you learn things about each other, but you will have a chance to become *curious* with your desires. This is a tool to support you in this process of figuring it out. When you take the opportunity to turn insight into action, your relationship and sexual health will grow.

The more you go for what you want and get it, the more you build the confidence to keep going for it. You are the expert of your sexual desire!

4. WOMEN NEED NOVELTY. WE GET BORED EASILY

Men don't always get us, and that's okay. A lot of men think women work the way that they do when it comes to getting turned on. Of course, that is not true. Men are very different and will not instinctively know how to turn a woman on. Many men come into their marriage thinking that going right into touching a woman in her erogenous zones (breasts, inner thigh, vulva, etc.) is how to get her turned on. While that may have worked the first few times when that was new and your touch was not familiar, it definitely does not work for long for most women.

If you walked up to your man and looked at him with wanting in your eyes and started to rub his crotch, he would probably be ready for sex in no time. But most women don't work that way, and you get to help your spouse understand that.

You get to share with your husband what non-sexual touch, what acts of service or gifts, what words, and what conversations help you feel safe, comfortable, wanted, and begin to turn you on outside the bedroom, well before he can go for the hot spots.

Women get bored. Our bodies get bored. We need novelty. A woman's body can predict what's next and doing the same thing every time does not keep us excited. Men think, "I did A, B, then C last time, and it worked! I'll just do that every time!" But the next few times he does that, it gets more and more predictable, and the result is definitely not the same as it was the first time.

Change and novelty are important for both men and women. Women like their man to change things up. The order of touch and the way we are touched all affect how that touch can impact our arousal and desire.

Women are much like water flowing in a river. Water can run over a piece of land for hundreds or thousands of years before it forms a canyon. Women respond similarly. Anything that a man does, he should do slower, knowing that it takes time to actually take effect. It takes women a long time to warm up, but we can also stay turned on for longer and have multiple orgasms.

Men are like fire. They burn through the forest quickly. They are turned on quickly, usually orgasm quicker than women, and then their desire is extinguished right after orgasm (well, at least for several hours or sometimes days).

5. EMBRACE YOUR SEXUALITY

Sexuality is a big part of who we are as human beings. It's written in our DNA, it's a driving force, and it can be a source of enormous pleasure. If this part of you is not nurtured and stimulated, your health suffers —there are mental, emotional, and physical consequences to denying or suppressing your sexuality.

Getting in touch with your sexuality is not as simple as turning on a faucet. It's about making a commitment to explore yourself, your desires, and how to respond to stimulation—in all ways. It can take time, but it's a process that can lead you to enormous pleasure and deeper connection.

> "Sexuality is a profound expression of yourself to another, a way of knowing and being known. It requires people to be comfortable with their bodies and with their sexuality."
>
> --Dr. Jennifer Finlayson-Fife, Ph.D.

I've found this visual (on the following page) to be very helpful, as it lets me see healthy sexuality displayed in a new way. This visual also came from Kristin Hodson's Instagram account @kristinbhodson

As you can see, the outer circles show aspects of our lives that affect our sexuality and when one or more are being affected our sexuality becomes unhealthy and our perception is skewed. But if we can work on each one, one at a time, we begin to find balance and meaning within our own sexuality.

6. BECOME A SEXUALLY ACTIVE AND AWARE WOMAN

Being a sexually active and aware woman does not mean you are "bad" or "naughty"—it simply means you are alive!

I am making one request: that you consider the significance and importance of your sexuality in terms of who you are. Don't compare yourself to your friends, your sister(s), your mother, or your daughter. Simply get to know your body, your mind, and your sexuality.

When I was reading *Come As You Are*, I resonated with a comparison about how no two snowflakes are the same. So it is with your sexuality and desire. No two are the same.

Would you rather embrace this powerful dimension of what makes you a woman and let it lead you to a wonderful, full life, or let it stay hidden and untapped, weighing you down in body and spirit?

7. REFER TO STEP 2, IN THE FEMALE SEXUAL RESPONSE CYCLE IN CHAPTER EIGHT

When I fully embraced that it was my responsibility to figure out what turns me on, it became easier to communicate with Trent what I do and don't like. Go through the Female Sexual Response Cycle and pay attention to the section on arousal. Begin to have conversations and share in a loving way what your husband does that helps and what he does that hinders your arousal. When you come from a place of love and wanting to enhance your sex, he should be more receptive (especially if he knows you'll be having better, more pleasurable sex together).

CHAPTER ELEVEN

I NEVER WANT IT...
IS THAT NORMAL?

"I don't understand why, but I really find it difficult to want to have sex with my husband."

How many of you have said that in your mind over and over again? I remember those days. You just don't get excited about wanting to have sex with him. The first 16 years of my marriage, I felt bad that I asked that question time and time again. I didn't know what the problem was. I thought maybe I was broken, or something was wrong with me. Plus, I felt bad for him too, and how it made him feel less wanted.

Why was it hard for me to keep the thrill and excitement over time? Many of us women wonder if there is something wrong with us. We want to feel normal. Then it may get to the point where you don't even feel attracted to your spouse anymore, and it becomes easier to ignore the problem. Then you convince yourself that you don't need sex, or that you just aren't sexual.

Or you really do love him, and you are attracted to him; you just always find reasons not to have sex.

This type of scenario is not uncommon. I found this in myself and my lack of sexual desire was a symptom of another underlying difficulty that I hadn't yet discovered.

Women say they need to:

- Feel in the mood for sex

- Feel connected to their spouse

- Feel loved and cherished by their spouse

- Feel attractive, sexy, or desirable

- Feel wanted or desired by their spouse

- Have a romantic environment

While this is what women may say and believe, I will share again, as mentioned under "desire" in Chapter Eight, that research from scientists and sexologists have shown that desire depends on 3 things:

1. An ability to become aroused

2. A healthy attitude toward sex

3. Proper sexual function (healthy sex organs)

So, when a woman is experiencing low libido or loss of desire, one of these three components has more than likely been impacted.

I had all three of them impacted at one point or another, but for sure the ability to become aroused and a healthy attitude toward sex were my top two issues for many years!

Which one of those three components are being impacted for you to have a low desire for sex?

WHAT CHANGED MY PERCEPTION

1. MY NORMAL IS NOT LIKE YOUR NORMAL

You want to know the biggest questions we ask ourselves about everything we do with sex?

- Is what I am doing normal?
- Is this the correct way to do this?
- Am I normal?
- What's the normal amount of times we should be having sex?

Everyone wants to know that they are normal. Sure, there are statistics out there, but it is not as helpful to do what is statistical. You also will find that the more you understand your body, what turns you on, and as your attitude towards sex changes, your "normal" will change and likely increase.

For me, I went from only wanting sex on very rare occasion a couple of times a year to wanting it at least one or two times a week. What is or was normal for me is not your normal, so don't worry about what I did, or do or what others tell you is "normal' for them. It can help to try things others have tried-just don't expect that to be the only solution. Be comfortable with where you are as you figure out what is best and normal for your relationship.

2. YOU CAN MOVE FROM NO DESIRE TO GREAT DESIRE

We've been hearing a lot about how women have no desire for sex. I'd like to turn that around! The more you understand the connection between your body, your libido, your mind, and your ability to become aroused, the more in control of your sexuality you will become.

Low libido is not the end; let us choose to see it as a starting point. And it's my sincere belief that with more information and more understanding, women will feel more confident and in control of what may always have been a vast unknown area.

Keep in mind, too, that it is up to you to figure out what turns you on as was discussed in Chapter Ten. When women come to me and complain, "My spouse does not know what he's doing!" I always remind them that men are not born knowing how to please us, and we were not born knowing what gives us pleasure.

You get to start by discovering your own path to sensation, and then you can begin to communicate this to your spouse. Together you get to learn new things, even if you've been together for 30+ years.

3. EXPECTATIONS KILL YOUR DESIRE AND YOUR RELATIONSHIPS

Expectations are any thoughts you have about any aspect or detail of a situation, especially around sex. When you anticipate something, have an opinion about it, or have feelings related to it, you begin to create an expectation of what you will experience.

It's a natural part of how your brain works--comparing experiences you are having to what you have experienced before, either by yourself directly or based on what others have told you.

Expectations set you up for wonderment or for disappointment. They basically tell your brain not only what it should want, but also to be unsatisfied if you don't get what you expect.

Unfortunately, expectations are commonly to blame for sexual dissatisfaction on both sides. Humans have a large layer of emotion and meaning that is attached to our sexual interactions, and this significantly shapes our thoughts, preferences, and desires.

Many of these ideas are passed on in our culture, through our family, through images and messages in advertising and movies, and through what we learn from religion, teachers and friends. Each person also has their own personal level of meaning for what is a turn on and what is appropriate during sex. Their individual fantasies, wants, and pleasures are shaped by these. All of these can contribute to expectations that alter your experiences by creating a filter so that the brain only pays attention or gives importance to the particular behaviors, characteristics, or meanings it is looking for.

One of the main difficulties with sexual expectations is that they are often unrealistic. When you see couples portraying how "in love" they are, it's almost impossible to compare your relationship to theirs. You know all the problems in your relationship but can only seem to see the good things in their relationship. Reality shows, movies, or even social media are all areas where we tend to compare and set up unrealistic expectations.

What happens then is that people's expectations of what relationships should be like become based on what they think other people are experiencing or feeling.

It is normal for your brain to behave this way. It is searching its environment to see what others are doing and then seeing how you measure up.

But the realities of day-to-day life include sorrow, imperfection, struggles, compromises, and boredom. People's lives are filled with downtime, routine, and effort. Real life is not usually the things glorified and promoted on reality TV or social media. Sex is no exception.

Unrealistic expectation can affect your sex life by influencing your ideas about sex directly, as well as by how you think the nature of your relationship with your spouse should be. With the expectation that your spouse will be all things to you at all times, you can easily get disillusioned that maybe they aren't the right one for you, or that you are missing out.

4. PLEASURE IN SEX IS ALSO FOR ME

As I began to want to have sex, I found it was mostly because I chose to have a healthy attitude toward sex. I learned through the many books I read that understanding how the brain learns, reacts, and changes over time depended more on my patterns of thinking and my patterns of behavior than anything else.

There are several dimensions of sexual desire outside the physical that have to align for healthy sexual desire, such as what you have learned about what's appropriate (sexually), how you feel about yourself (sexually), and what you interpret in your spouse as being 'sexy' or a turn on.

As I began to look deep into my own sexual dysfunction I asked the question,

"What was draining my desire for sex?"

For me, I found that a big part of this was my lack of focus on *my* pleasure! *My* ability to become aroused. All I wanted to focus on with my husband when we were having sex was *his* pleasure. I never focused on mine! I was not selfish when having sex. I wanted to make it good for him and move on.

Pleasure itself is an awesome reward for any activity, especially sex! But what happens in your brain when there is less pleasure, or when you are distracted from pleasure? It makes for a difficult sexual experience. People often underestimate the effect that diminished sexual pleasure has on our sexual desire. When we don't focus on our pleasure during sex, when we think about our to-do list or just focus on helping our husband "finish," we start to make false associations and see sex as not fun, not pleasurable. Of course we wouldn't want more sex if this is the case!

Most people look for the physical reasons why their desire has fizzled out. I sure did! Of course there are physical reasons for a low desire or libido (reference the section on "desire" in Chapter Eight, *The Female*

Sexual Response Cycle for the list of things that can affect your desire).

When I started being more selfish during sex (Trent actually really enjoys it when I am focused on receiving pleasure, and you may find your husband feels the same way--good men really want to sexually pleasure their wives), I noticed that I could orgasm quicker, I could orgasm multiple times, I could experience more intense orgasms, and I started desiring sex and connection with Trent like never before. Focus on your own pleasure, and you will start to see a change. Now, let's talk about how your brain can help you do that!

5. YOUR BRAIN IS YOUR GATEKEEPER

Everything that you are taught about sex and sexuality from the time you are young and even today helps make up your ideas, views, and beliefs about sex. I'll refer to them as your "beliefs about sex" like I talked about in Chapter One. Learning what is sexy versus what is disgusting is something that happens in your childhood and teen years, shaping the list of what will become a "turn on" or a "turn off" for you. These beliefs about sex and what is sexy versus what isn't are heavily shaped by culture and by how others around you respond to different aspects of sex and sexuality.

These beliefs about sex even affect how you think of your body and your sexual functioning--whether something is appropriate or not--which then affects how much pleasure you allow yourself to feel.

Because your brain processes every bit of information it receives, consciously or subconsciously, it acts as a gatekeeper to the deeper parts of your primitive brain where sexual arousal is controlled. The thinking part of your brain decides if something is sexy or not, and then either allows the arousal process to continue, or short circuits it.

Your thinking brain is controlling your sexual desire! In fact, it's the one that decides if it's okay for you to have desire, and whether or not you deserve it. It also tells you if you should feel guilty for having desire. These are just some of the ways that the thinking brain can rule and also ruin your sex life.

When it comes to the social dimension of desire, the physical reality of being tired and stressed will have a negative impact on your body, but so will anger or distance from your spouse. Outside factors will come in too, such as your desire to impress your boss at your job. Recognizing each of these details helps you decide which factor needs to be addressed first, or if any or all can be overcome at that moment.

So you see, you are much more complex when it comes to your sexuality and sexual desire. You do have more control than you previously believed. You can choose to analyze false beliefs that may have held you back until now. You can choose to be open to curiosity about your body, your arousal, and desire. You can choose to suspend some beliefs while you choose to experience deep connection and pleasure with your husband. In the chapter on the Female Sexual Response Cycle, you'll notice that the first step is about *your* choice. It's not about waiting for your husband to do just the right things (although that will help, and you get to teach him what those things are as you explore and understand what gets your turned on) It is about your choice and deciding to want to experiment with more pleasure and connection with your husband. Deciding you are worthy of pleasure and deserve pleasure and sexual connection.

6. YOUR BRAIN IS YOUR LARGEST SEX ORGAN

It's up to you. Go inside your brain.

The brain is the largest sexual organ in the body. However, the brain-body response for female arousal is more complicated than for male arousal.

How we feel about ourselves, our spouses, and our lives in general is a key factor in arousal during sexual activity. Sexual response is a complicated reaction that does indeed begin within the brain. Therefore sexual health also includes mental health!

What do you do to take care of your mind?

Sure, having great sex and becoming a great lover is about technique. But only partly. It's also about going inside yourself and being fully present. It's about letting yourself become aware of every inch of your body and paying attention to how your body responds to touch, to music, to kissing, to whatever is happening to or around you.

It's also about giving that same attention to your spouse.

Try something right now. Read this paragraph and then close your eyes and let yourself travel in your mind. Imagine yourself on a beach. Can you feel the soft breeze on your face and your arms? Can you feel the sand between your toes? Can you hear the rhythm of the waves as the surf comes in? Can you smell the salty air? Now pause for a moment and really sink into this mental picture.

If you are able to let your mind travel, and if you are able to imagine the above sensual experiences, then you can certainly bring that same attention and heightened awareness to your lovemaking. It is a choice.

Having wonderful sex is much more about being fully engaged in what you are doing than it is about any technique you can perform. It is about choosing to be present and connect your brain to what your body desires. It is about connecting your brain to the sensation of your vulva and vagina changing, expanding or contracting as you become aroused. It is about focusing your mind on the pleasure your clitoris, vulva, and vagina experience as you are in your favorite sexual positions for the right pressure and the right rhythm and tempo. Your brain and focus on your pleasure control all of this. If you find yourself being blocked by other thoughts or distractions, begin training your mind to come back into focus on your pleasure and your desire.

7. REFER TO STEP 3, DESIRE, IN THE FEMALE SEXUAL RESPONSE CYCLE IN CHAPTER EIGHT

Sex is a mind game and it will test your mental strength. Once you can get a handle on wanting to want sex, over time you will train your mind to relax and not think of the long laundry list of what affects your desire that I mentioned in Chapter Eight.

CHAPTER TWELVE

WHY DOES MY SPOUSE WANT IT SO MUCH MORE THAN ME?

I'm sure you've had plenty of conversations around this topic with your spouse, am I right? Mismatched sex drives are frequently a cause for disagreement in marriage. I know for me it was a real problem. I didn't understand why Trent felt like he needed more sex than I did, and I didn't want to talk about our differences is sex drive. I didn't think sex was that important--and I never wanted to think about sex. I wished he would just adopt my way of thinking and perspective that having sex a few times a month was good enough.

We tend to only see our side of the sex drive debate and often demonize our spouse for their higher or lower desire for sex. Some of us even adopt the belief that our spouse is either intentionally withholding love or is trying to control us.

I don't like using "high sex drive" and "low sex drive" to describe spouses in a marriage relationship. In my marriage, I am the one who desires sex less frequently. I would be referred to as the low sex drive spouse. The issue I have with this terminology is that it sounds like my libido is off or that something is wrong with me. The truth is that I currently desire sex more often than ever before in my marriage and more than many men, so if I was married to someone else, I suddenly would be labeled as the "high sex drive" partner.

I've found a new description of these differences in sex drive that I like better. Jay Dee is a blogger and coach at UncoveringIntimacy.com who focuses on marriage and intimacy. He shared this about sex drive differences:

"When you call your spouse "low-drive," or someone else refers to them that way, they start to internalize it. It becomes a self-fulfilling prophecy of sorts. They believe and adopt the role.

It also creates another negative tie to sex. Them being "low-drive" becomes associated with sex, so it's a more difficult topic to discuss, because it brings to mind this perception of being inadequate."

--Jay Dee, UncoveringIntimacy.com

For the remainder of the book I will use these new terms instead of referring to you or your spouse as "low sex drive" or "high sex drive." The terms are as follows:

Sexual pursuer – the one who tends to pursue by default, who spontaneously desires sex more often.

Sexual responder – the one who tends to take a more receptive role when it comes to sex, for whatever reason.

The benefit of not labeling someone as "low sex drive" is that they don't see themselves as broken. Feeling broken is common among many women I work with, as they feel they don't match up to their spouse's expectations. They aren't turned on by the same things; they don't usually think about sex often, if at all, and they don't initiate sex often.

When the labels are changed to pursuer instead of high sex drive and responder instead of low sex drive, we can remove the negative feeling of being compared and labeled as above or below (higher or lower) when compared to our partner. A marriage between a pursuer and a responder can definitely be a marriage where it's possible to coexist and have an amazing sex life together.

Two sexual responders in a marriage will often have less arguments about the frequency of sex, but there are still going to be some differences in desire and drive, as no two humans will desire sex at the same time, every time. They also still have disagreements about sex, and they often have differences in what turns them on and what gets them warmed up for sex.

Likewise, two sexual pursuers in a marriage aren't likely to be free from sexual frustrations, either. Again, frequency of sex may not be a point of disagreement, but they still are not guaranteed to be happy and in perfect harmony.

All relationships are different, and yours might not match my examples below, but I have chosen to focus this chapter on the most common scenario: the husband is the sexual pursuer and the wife is the sexual responder. If you are flip-flopped, adjust some of the suggestions, and you will begin to see more harmony replace the arguments or frustration around differing levels of interest in sex.

I've asked Trent to share his perspective on being a pursuer. I've found this matches up very closely to what I've heard from the couples we've worked with and the conversations with husbands specifically.

"Like many men, I feel that the quality and frequency of sex in my marriage is a way for me to gauge how things are going. When we feel like we are connecting frequently through sex and we feel our spouse is showing interest and enjoying having sex, we feel that our relationship is in a good place. It doesn't mean

that sex is the only thing we value, or that it is all we want out of our marriage; it is just something we use as a test of, 'are we still good?' It can help us know when something is off in our relationship. This isn't necessarily right or wrong, it just is how many sexual pursuers feel.

A few years ago, when I was feeling hurt and not confident in our relationship, I would approach sex timidly. I would slowly test the waters and only initiate sex if I was 100% certain Sarah would respond positively. This timid approach came from not knowing if I was going to be rejected and turned away, as I didn't understand why Sarah didn't want to have sex very often and what I was or wasn't doing to affect her desire. I had learned to avoid that pain of rejection, as I interpreted it to mean I wasn't wanted. It came from me not having the emotional intelligence to communicate my needs and wants in a healthy way. It came from interpreting her response in that moment as a representation of how much she did or didn't love me.

A pursuer wants to feel desired and accepted by their spouse, and sex is their preferred way to feel that. If a pursuer is frequently rejected, they may internalize that to mean their spouse is saying, "I don't want you" or "I don't love you." The more frequently this happens, the more likely the pursuer will believe this negative belief, even if it is not the intention of their spouse to make them feel this way.

What I learned is that I was often being selfish by expecting Sarah to simply respond to my desire for sex. I learned that I wasn't working with her on warming her up with my words and actions. I wasn't thinking of how to emotionally connect with her and bring safety and security to her mind so that she would be open and receptive to connect with me through sex."

When a husband and wife learn how to show love in their spouse's preferred love language, and when they are able to communicate their individual wants and needs in a clear way, pursuers and responders begin to feel more aligned. For this to work for Trent and me, we shared with each other how it was important for me to be warmed up and pursued properly by him, and that it would make us both feel better. We also talked about how increasing my receptivity to the possibility of sex would make him feel better. By respecting our differences and working on serving each other, more comfort, peace, connection, and security came into our marriage.

When a pursuer learns that in order for the responder to respond positively, it requires some effort on their part, it can change the marriage. A pursuer can't just show up and say, "I worked hard today to provide for the family, now I want sex," and expect the responder to be ready and in the mood. A sexual pursuer who has confidence and clarity has learned or asked ahead of time what they can do to prepare the responder, and actively works at doing those things that will assist their responder spouse to be in a good state of mind and feeling emotionally connected. The wise sexual pursuer knows this does not guarantee anything, but increases the chances their spouse will be a willing responder the next time the pursuer wants to initiate sex.

Now, a few words about sexual responders. Most--but not all--sexual responders are women. You likely think about sex on rare occasions, and if you are like I was a few years ago, you only think about it while in the act. Many sexual responders don't feel like they desire sex often, as they usually are satisfied with the amount of sex they are having. This is why it is rare for responders to initiate sex.

The issue that many sexual responders find, even when working on increasing the frequency and their mental presence during sex, is that it often still falls short of their spouse's expectations for more frequent and more passionate sex. This can trigger thoughts like, "I'll never be good enough," or "why bother, it doesn't seem to make a difference." I personally had begun to feel that Trent was just selfish and that no matter what I did, I wouldn't be able to match his level of interest.

After many long conversations about how we act and react as both pursuer and responder, it was clear to Trent and me what the solution was to our mismatched levels of interest in and desire for sex. It required a bit of effort at first and some difficult changes from both of us. This combined effort has been the catalyst for changing our marriage and our love and connection. In the sections below, I'll share what worked for us.

WHAT CHANGED MY PERCEPTION

1. SEX DRIVE DIFFERENCES AREN'T THE PROBLEM

Trent and I have had many conversations that helped us understand each other and compromise on things. At the same time, we feel more love and connection as we better understand and serve each other. Loving spouses don't try to force the other to change. They focus on understanding each other and then meeting each other's needs.

As you understand each other better, you will be able to modify your frequency to better match with your individual desires. You may also notice that by better improving warm-up and foreplay, as well as addressing any shame as discussed in this book, the sexual responder spouse may experience their sexual desire start to increase.

Differing views on frequency of sex requires some compromise. When you both work on understanding each other and focus on serving your spouse with love, these differences become less of an issue, as both of your needs will begin to be met more often.

2. LEARN THE TRUTH ABOUT THE SEXUAL RESPONDER

The truth is that the sexual responder spouse rarely thinks about sex. They shouldn't be expected to be spontaneously in the mood, to think like the sexual pursuer spouse, or to desire sex or anything to do with it as much as the pursuer does. There's a good chance they'll be less interested in reading blog posts or books about sex or discussing new positions and activities.

When they're less interested in sex, it likely has less to do with a lack of interest in their spouse and more to do with the context of when the pursuer is initiating sex. It doesn't mean they don't love you; it just means that sex may not be on their radar and is not their primary way of showing love, nor likely their favorite way of being shown that they are loved. They're usually going to push their spouse to find non-sexual ways to be intimate and connect. That can be a good thing when it is communicated and the pursuer spouse understands they are still loved, even if it was not expressed through sex that time. However, if the responder spouse always defaults to non-sexual ways to show love, over time the problems I have discussed in this book will be present. Resentment and bitterness from always feeling like they are being teased, led along, but not feeling loved or wanted will build up for the sexual pursuer.

As the sexual responder in our marriage, here is what I decided to do. I asked questions, I listened, and I tried to understand how the quality and frequency of sex made Trent feel and affected him. I remained curious to understand the level of connection that he feels both physically and emotionally when we have sex during which I am present and wanting to experience pleasure with him. I decided to choose to want sex more often. Most responders may not realize this, but sex is a choice for us. When I started to choose this, I could start to warm up and prepare for foreplay with Trent. I even choose to start initiating sex a few times a month. I began to study and curiously experiment with what would help me be more relaxed and feel emotionally connected to Trent, so I would more likely to respond positively to him initiating sex.

I shared with Trent what I needed in order to feel relaxed, loved, and supported. This included sharing with him what I learned about the Female Sexual Response Cycle (see Chapter Eight) and things he could do to help me into and through the first two stages of warm up and foreplay/arousal. He knows that through his acts of service, I feel loved and supported. I hate doing dishes and cleaning bathrooms, so he does that as one way to lighten my load and express love to me in my love language.

Trent already knows that I am not ready for sex as quickly or as often as he is. I shared what he can do to help me prepare for sex by thinking of ways to show me love through service. He can do this by playing with the kids, by making me feel safe, by talking with me and listening to all the things floating around in my head. He knows now that by letting me clear my thoughts and share what is on my mind, I can relax and feel safe. This allows me to be in the mood for sex more often. He also knows that he doesn't need to fix these things that I share unless I ask for solutions. The last thing we agreed on was that acts of service, being more present with the kids, helping clear my mind, and other expressions of love don't always end in sex.

Assuming you are the sexual responder spouse, discuss with your husband ways he can help you feel more desire to connect sexually. Share how he can help you feel safe, appreciated for your contribution to the family, respected, desired, understood, and cherished. If you have identified your primary love language, share a practical way he can express love to you in that way on a daily or weekly basis. Express with as much detail as possible how it makes you feel when he shows you love in these ways. Often, men will go above and beyond if they understand how it makes you feel.

Help him understand that those things don't always lead to sex, but that it will help increase the frequency and the quality of your sex. Marriage and sex aren't a tally sheet, and we don't keep score or get to tell our spouse what they owe us. However, if you are the sexual responder and your husband is consistently serving you, sacrificing for you, and then constantly feeling let down that you don't want to connect with him, resentment and bitterness often will start to creep in.

3. SEXUAL PURSUERS ARE PASSIONATE ABOUT PASSION

The sexual pursuer spouse is going to think about sex more often. It doesn't mean they love the sexual responder spouse any less, or that "all they want is sex." It means that this is how they experience love in a very real and tangible way. Initiating sex is their way of saying "I love you," and sex is a way to spend time with the love of their life without barriers.

They're going to be more interested in making sex better, having sex more often, and generally are more excited about sex. It doesn't mean that sex isn't good the way it is, or that it's the only time they're satisfied with their spouse. It just means they're interested in sex and are always going to be looking to improve that connection they feel from sex with their spouse.

Sexual pursuers can improve the way they ask for sex. For example, instead of asking, "Do you want to have sex?" it would be better to ask, "are you open to having sex?" The second way of asking is respecting their spouse's agency, while the first often makes a responder think, "well, no, I don't actually," as that is probably their current state of mind unless the pursuer has already helped them warm up.

As the pursuer, here is what Trent decided to do. He listened and asked questions with curiosity to understand that when I wasn't in the mood for sex, that it didn't mean I didn't love him or that he wasn't good enough. Sometimes things were just not feeling right, and he knows that is okay. I communicated the way I felt when he pressured me to have sex when I wasn't feeling prepared. I shared with him the things I was learning about that would help me warm up and how slowly building up desire through foreplay really helps me want to connect with him.

What most helped me understand why both the frequency and quality of our sex was important to Trent was reading the book I mentioned previously, *For Women Only* by Shaundi Feldhahn, Social Researcher. Quality and frequency are important to Trent because he feels loved, respected, and connected through sex. Saying, "I appreciate your hard work," or cleaning the house or making dinner just don't express love to him in the same way. I also learned that he doesn't just want to have sex with my body. He wants me to be present and he wants to please me. This means that by choosing to be present with him and wanting to enjoy our intimate time together, I can express my love to him.

Ask your husband how often he prefers to have sex per week or per month. Secondly, ask why this frequency is important to him and how it makes him feel. Discuss how it feels when he tries to serve you, to show you love and respect, only to be let down that you don't want to be with him sexually. This can be a tough conversation, but try not to attack or defend your position; instead, remain curious, and try to understand each other's perspective.

Discuss with your spouse as either responder and pursuer how you prefer to communicate that you want to have sex so it is less of a turn off and feels less like an obligation.

CHAPTER THIRTEEN

I FEEL LIKE
I'M BROKEN

Have you ever had sex where you didn't orgasm, but your husband did? I'm sure you'll be able to recall several such incidents. Replay one in your mind. Really, truly take a few concentrated moments and think about how you felt (ex. unsurprised, neutral, disappointed, worked, upset), and why you think you felt that way.

Now reverse the scenario.

Have you ever had sex where you had an orgasm and your husband didn't? If not, imagine the scenario. Either way, real or imagined, take another few moments to genuinely examine how you felt and why you felt this way. If you felt more negative about his lack of orgasm than your own lack of orgasm, you're still at least partially buying into the belief that your husband's orgasms are more important than yours.

You are not broken. Women have been programmed to think that their sexual pleasure is secondary to a man's. You might also believe, in whole or in part, that if we don't orgasm from penetration, every time we have sex, something might be wrong with us.

So, what's the solution? You need to truly believe that your sexual pleasure is of utmost importance. It means feeling entitled to pleasure. I know some might have a negative reaction to the word entitled, because it makes you sound selfish. But I'm not using the word entitled in the way you think I am. Feeling entitled to pleasure means believing that it's essential that your husband cares about your pleasure, that you both genuinely believe that your pleasure is as important as his. This means you expect him to consider stimulating your clitoris to be as central to sex as stimulating his penis. In other words, entitlement could simply be another way of saying equality.

Many women and some men experience difficulty reaching orgasm. Just as men need sufficient stimulation of the penis to climax or ejaculate, women need sufficient stimulation of the clitoris to reach orgasm.

I was blessed to not struggle with reaching orgasm. It comes very easily for me when I choose to be sexual. My hang-up was that after I experienced an orgasm, I would have immediate guilt that I allowed my body to have such an intense, pleasurable experience. This guilt was due to my conditioning in my head about sex and that I had just done something *bad*.

To overcome this feeling of guilt, I began to shut down my desire for sex. I didn't want to feel guilty, so although I could orgasm if I chose to, I would instead choose to either lay there and not be involved in sex, or I would fake it. I thought that by faking it, Trent could feel good about giving me pleasure and I could avoid feeling guilty since I didn't do anything bad. How messed up is that!? I became really good at fake orgasms. Come on, I'm sure many of you have done it a time or two or 50.

Another way about 10% of women (Study by Kim Wallen, Ph.D. and Elisabeth A. Lloyd, Ph.D. on female sexual arousal) feel broken is from not being able to reach orgasm. Most cases of failure to attain orgasm that I have read about and discussed with women who I coach began with poor preparation for marriage or sex. This usually also created a frustrating and fearful honeymoon, followed by a prolonged period of disappointment and boredom in marriage that conditioned the woman to feel there was no hope for fulfillment. Feeling broken is common at that point. Then, they began to resent their husbands because orgasm came easy for them or because they feel guilty from having an orgasm with their husband (like I would), so they learned to shut down their sex altogether.

In my work of teaching sexual health to women, I have met women who have *never* experienced an orgasm. Some of you reading this right now are thinking, "yep, that's me." The first time I heard that from a woman, I felt sad that she had been married for several years and not yet experienced this deep, intense pleasure that I had taken for granted and had shut down for years. She felt broken.

If you find yourself in either area (felt guilt or shame from experiencing pleasure or don't experience orgasm at all), let me be the first to tell you that you're not broken. There is hope in most cases to overcome the feeling of shame or guilt and to begin to feel pleasure and reach orgasm.

One thing that works against orgasm is anxiety. This is true for both men and women. The more anxious you are, the less likely you are to reach your orgasm threshold.

For example, if you are feeling pressure because your spouse is impatient or bored during sex, or if you feel responsible for performing so your husband feels like he has done his job (giving you pleasure), or if you are feeling self-conscious about your body, state of arousal or anything else, it will be very challenging to orgasm. The very thought of trying to orgasm when you haven't before will make it almost impossible to reach orgasm.

If there is anything creating anxiety around sex, it is important to work on that and discuss it with your husband. If you have had sexual trauma, this may not be something you can overcome just by talking with your spouse. You should consider finding a therapist who can help you through the anxiety that is attached to this past trauma.

It is rare to find a woman who is incapable of an orgasm when she is properly stimulated and there are not any limiting physical or medical issues. I know that just reading that might sting for some of you. You may feel like you've tried everything and you've given up hope. I've worked with several women now who have gone from years of not being able to orgasm, to being able to reach climax and experience intense pleasure for the first time because they were taught the importance of relaxation and proper stimulation.

There is much more to it, as each case and each person is unique, but hold on to that hope that you are likely in that group of women that are capable of orgasm, even if you haven't yet experienced it. You are not broken. It is a matter of identifying what beliefs might be creating anxiety, what beliefs might be creating shame or guilt, and then working on analyzing and adjusting those beliefs that are holding you back from enjoying sex. Next, you get to work on identifying what would properly help you relax, warm up, and become aroused.

Finally, look around and discover what tools exist to help you increase your brain-body connection so you can receive and accept proper stimulation to bring you to orgasm. There are enhancement creams and bedroom accessories that can assist you in making that pleasure connection between your brain and clitoris.

One thing that you may have noticed, which affects men and women, is that when sexual energy and tension are not satisfactorily or fully released, this can cause anger or frustration, a dislike of lovemaking, and resentment toward your spouse.

If a woman has difficulty reaching orgasm as quickly as her man does, sometimes this mental and physical block to reaching climax is actually coming from the subconscious mind. One philosophy is that women may subconsciously be testing men to see if he is patient enough and will stick with it long enough to please his woman. Will he reach orgasm before us and then move on or fall asleep? This ability to focus on his woman's pleasure and stick with it shows that he has patience. Patience is a quality needed in creating and raising a family. We want to know that he is patient enough to be with us in the long run, to take care of us and our family.

For those of you who are indifferent or don't care as much about reaching orgasm, I hope you will recognize that there are benefits to figuring out your sexual desire and what stimulates you. This will not only strengthen your relationship with your husband but will also physically promote well-being for you.

For women who are stimulated and aroused, but for whatever reason don't orgasm, each time she fails to reach orgasm, this represents some injury to the pelvic organs and to her emotions, often leaving her with nervousness, weakness, fatigue, and can also manifest in some pelvic and low back pain. It is worth exploring and being open to the belief that orgasm is possible for you.

WHAT CHANGED MY PERCEPTION

1. FOCUS ON YOURSELF

This is the one of the best times to be selfish in your relationship. Ladies, you must be willing to *receive* during lovemaking if you want to *give* the greatest pleasure to your man. We focus so much on giving in our day-to-day lives as wives, mothers, and sisters that we forget to receive.

I once heard from a speaker at a seminar, "Always giving and never receiving is like only exhaling and never inhaling." Learn to inhale and accept and receive.

> *"One of the reasons that many of us don't like to receive is we like the control of being the giver."*
> --Dr. Jennifer Finlayson-Fife, Ph.D.

Let go of controlling how you are giving and focus on receiving.

Being self-focused sexually can help women achieve orgasm. One of the greatest gifts wives can give their husbands is to be sexually satisfied. A good man's greatest sexual fulfillment comes from lighting the fire of desire in his wife and watching it blow up into flames of passion and pleasure. If you don't believe me, just ask your husband.

2. LEARNING ABOUT MY ANATOMY AND MY OWN BODY

As I began to read content from dozens of books about the female anatomy, sex, arousal, and orgasm, it opened my mind, and I saw that it was safe and okay to learn about my body. I was allowed to find out how my body works, what areas are used for sex and pleasure, and how to enhance that. I finally realized (as silly as this might sound) that sex and having intense pleasure with my husband is natural and God-given.

Becoming cliterate is all about being literate as to how your clitoris works says, Laurie Mintz, author of *Becoming Clierate*. This means learning what brings you pleasure and believing that you have the right to such pleasure.

I was blown away to learn that women were created with an organ with the sole purpose of feeling pleasure. The clitoris is God's gift to women. Did God do that by accident or by design? I believe I was designed to receive pleasure. God created us as sexual beings and wants me to be a sexual and fully connected with Trent in the most intimate and powerful way possible. Through sex, I am designed to be pleasured by my husband with his body.

The clitoris is the most sensitive tissue on the woman's body, and it is just the tip of a larger five to six inch structure that extends back up into the body and branches around the urethra and vagina. The inner structure of the clitoris includes a shaft and two branches (called *Crus Clitoris* - also described as roots or legs) of erectile tissue that extend up to five inches into the body on both sides of the vagina.

A man's penis has about 4,000 nerve endings. That's a lot. However, the penis is a dual-purpose organ and used for urination and for pleasure. A woman's clitoris, our hot spot of pleasure, has about double the nerve endings of a penis with over 8,000 nerve endings! Again, the clitoris's sole purpose is pleasure. So that means double the pleasure and double the fun! Let that sink in.

Does learning that your clitoris, that was designed by God, and was created with the sole purpose of allowing women to feel intense pleasure change your view and understanding of what sex can be for you?

Are you curious to know more about how you can connect this pleasure organ with your mind to create amazing, connected, pleasurable sexual experiences with your husband?

As I learned about my body and how the clitoris works, I saw a major shift in my thinking. Instead of judging sex and rejecting the possibility that I may actually enjoy myself, I succeeded in opening my mind and heart to learning about myself and what I wanted. Coming out of that place of negative association to sex and a closed mind, I now had a desire to explore.

Of course, I don't mean I was going to explore having sex with other people or go against other beliefs around what is proper in a married sexual relationship, as I can see and attest to the benefits of monogamy. But I was finally ready to explore pleasure with my husband in a curious and exploratory manner. I had awakened this side of myself that I feared would be "out of control" and realized those old fears were not based on truth.

What I found is that it has instead brought me more confidence, more stability, and more connection with my husband. I can finally explore my body along with my husband without shame, guilt, or judgement.

In this humorous and instructive animated documentary, learn about the clitoris' unrecognized anatomy. https://youtu.be/J_3OA_VZVkY

3. GET THE BOOK, SLOW SEX

A great book to read or listen to that would help with figuring out what sensations feel good is *Slow Sex*.

This guide taught Trent and I how to use the practice of Orgasmic Meditation--or OM--to slow down, connect emotionally, and achieve authentic female sexual satisfaction.

OM focuses exclusively on helping women to learn how to connect the sensations in the clitoris to their brain.

4. PAY ATTENTION TO PLEASURE ON YOUR CLITORIS & TRY DIFFERENT POSITIONS

Practice paying attention to the pleasure in your body. One way that I've found to stay present is to focus on my clitoris the entire time I am having sex.

Performance anxiety happens frequently, but if you can merely focus on the clitoris itself, then you'll be able to feel relaxed.

By focusing on the sensation you are feeling in that region of your body, you will find your mind has a big impact on your ability to feel pleasure. As you create a meditative focus on your clitoris, you can dial in on that pleasure point and maybe start to feel something new. Give that a try next time and see the difference it will make. This will help you to focus on your pleasure and be present. Trust me, it works!

One side of your clitoris is more sensitive than the other. Yes, it's true! That's your homework for tonight: go have sex to find out which side it is. It's just a fun fact.

Many women have found that the woman on top position gives them the most control of speed/tempo and pressure on the clitoris. If you are trying to feel more pleasure, try positions where you can control more and focus on finding your pleasure.

5. WOMEN CAN HAVE MULTIPLE ORGASMS

Women are different than men and they can have multiple orgasms.

For years, I had no idea it was even possible to have more than a clitoral orgasm, or that I could have multiple orgasms, one right after the other! As I've shared, I used to shut down and feel guilt right after I had an orgasm, so of course that shut me off from exploring and feeling more.

Once I learned that I could have multiple types of orgasms and that I could have multiples in the same love-making session, I began to explore. Oh boy! Once you open your mind to it, there are possibilities. I can easily have 2-4 orgasms every time we have sex if I really want to. Of course, working on your spouse's sexual endurance may be a limitation here, but if not, open your mind to it and start exploring today.

I won't go into explicit detail, but you can explore with manual, oral, and other types of stimulation with your spouse if that sounds more like your style! Sometimes having an orgasm from one type of stimulation will set you up for a second or third orgasm with the same or a different type of stimulation. Explore and communicate to find out what you enjoy.

What happens inside your body when an orgasm happens?

Blood flows into this pelvic area of your body as you are turned on. This extra blood facilitates orgasm and pleasure. Orgasm is a result of the body quickly pumping blood away from the sexual organs. Some women may experience some blood congestion in her vagina/vulva if she is aroused, but then doesn't orgasm. This is one reason why orgasm is important for women.

You've already read in Chapter Eight that there are five different types of orgasms you can experience: vaginal, clitoral, nipple, G-spot, and anal orgasms. What these really refer to are the types of stimulation that cause an orgasm.

There is really only *one* kind of orgasm, which is the physical reaction that the body has to certain types of stimulation.

6. LEARN HOW AN ORGASM HAPPENS TO KNOW IF YOU'VE FELT ONE

You may have heard, "If you don't know if you've had an orgasm, you probably haven't." This statement isn't especially useful for those of you wanting to experience one, so I'd like to give you a sense of what an orgasm is and feels like from Dr. Laurie Mintz. She states:

"To understand orgasms, remember engorgement, which is when those special capillaries in erectile tissue let blood in but not out. All that blood going into your erectile tissue creates tension that builds up to a high point. An orgasm is when powerful rhythmic muscle contractions release that tension. These muscles are called pelvic floor muscles and their contractions prevent additional blood from coming into your erectile tissue. When the contractions cease, blood flows in and out again, rather than just in, and your erectile tissue shrinks back to its original size and color."

For me it feels like all the tension that had been building and building is released with an explosion. But also at times it feels like riding a series of waves on a tidal wave. It is the most pleasurable thing in the world.

Many women feel the intense, pulsing muscle contraction of orgasm, yet others feel a general build-up of muscle tension followed by a pleasurable feeling of overall release.

7. REFER TO STEP 4, ORGASM, IN THE FEMALE SEXUAL RESPONSE CYCLE IN CHAPTER EIGHT

The goal when having sex is not necessarily to orgasm. The vast majority of women cannot orgasm from the stimulation provided by vaginal intercourse alone. The overwhelming majority of nerve endings that women need to reach orgasm are on the *outside*. Penetration is not required. Clitoral stimulation is. This is why truly appreciating and attending to the clitoris is the *simple secret* to your orgasm. When you remove the pressure to perform and achieve orgasm, you will enjoy sex more.

CHAPTER FOURTEEN

I DON'T KNOW ENOUGH ABOUT SEX SO I WON'T TALK ABOUT IT

Every woman wants an amazing, connected relationship with a good man who honors, loves and cherishes her like she sees in chick flicks. You know those Nicholas Sparks movies?

Come on, you know I'm right!

Sadly, this is the hope and dream most women lose over the years of marriage. It happened to me as I lost myself in my children and focused solely on them. I was so consumed with caring for my children that I didn't feel like I knew Trent anymore, and I didn't feel attracted to him.

I feared that my husband wouldn't love me as much if he knew the true, imperfect me. I truly had this fear, and over the first 12 years of our marriage, I wouldn't engage in meaningful, heartfelt conversations because I wanted to keep my wall up.

Unfortunately, most of us have been trained to show up in masks, to appear to be "perfect," or act as others expect us to act in order to be accepted and loved.

Then, because of my belief that I didn't know enough, I feared that Trent would think I'm not smart and capable. This would lead to me shutting down all communication.

I felt like I was not equal to my husband whenever he tried to talk about difficult things. I felt walked all over because the words that he shared with me made me think I didn't know enough. I would then of course shut down, not share my own thoughts, and just let it go. I would try to sweep it under the rug as if nothing ever happened.

On the inside, this belief that I didn't know enough grew and grew because I chose not to deal with my insecurities and communicate how I was really feeling. Trent had no intention of making me feel this way. When I finally addressed this, it brought him to tears to think how I interpreted his desire to communicate with me as him judging me as not smart enough and not an equal partner with him.

This lack of authentic communication not only happened in my marriage, but it also happened with my other relationships. I would just let people walk all over me and take advantage of me because I didn't want to communicate my own feelings, and I would just tell myself to get over it.

Deep down we each have a desire to be loved. Unfortunately, this desire causes us to do things in a way that actually impedes our opportunity to experience more love. When I believed "I am not good enough" or "I don't know enough," I would hide my true self from those I loved.

I pretended to be as everyone wanted me to be, because I thought that in order to be accepted and loved, I had to meet other's expectations.

I also noticed when I felt this way that I gave the impression to Trent that he wasn't good enough either. I would put him down about the things he wasn't doing for our family. At one point in our marriage, it was so bad that we were talking through emails instead of face-to-face. We didn't know how to communicate, and one or the other would have to walk away to avoid getting into an argument.

Poor communication results in poor relationships.

We all know this, and we hear it time and time again. When we are feeling judged, we forget how to react appropriately because we are so conditioned to react defensively when attacked or judged.

When one spouse isn't being authentic in their communication, then neither one tends to be authentic. If one is holding back, the other doesn't feel secure in being fully exposed and fully authentic. It is way easier for most people to be completely naked physically in front of their spouse than it is to be fully exposed, mentally and emotionally through their words.

The source of most of my struggles in marriage was because of our poor communication.

Poor communication meant that we didn't talk about sex either.

If Trent wanted to talk about it, I would shut him down and avoid it. I just didn't know how to effectively communicate about sex for sure, so I would retreat or hold back. Most often, this would come up at night when the kids were in bed, and I'd just roll over and pretend I was asleep.

I was often anxious about my own desires and didn't know how to share those with my husband. He desired me to have pleasure, but because I saw it as bad, I suppressed my desire.

I know that sounds weird, especially when you're married to someone, but that was the reality of my situation. We had never really spoken about it openly and our sex life just coasted along. I have even withheld sex because I was so angry at him. He didn't know why I felt this anger.

How many of you don't talk with your spouse about sex? Sometimes, it's part of a larger issue of not wanting to talk at all, but often, every other topic is acceptable--it's just sex that isn't.

Not talking about sex makes it seem undesirable. Typically, we don't like to talk about things that are dirty, or we otherwise don't want to deal with. "Bathroom talk" is an example of this. We all know we pee and poop, but talking about it is socially unacceptable, even more so than sex. Truth is that people don't really want to deal with what we do in the bathroom. They'd rather not have to deal with waste at all. Life would be better without it, and I truly believed that about sex. I just thought that if I didn't talk about it, it would go away, and I wouldn't desire it anymore.

Not talking about sex makes it seem sinful. I didn't talk to Trent about the things that I was doing that I knew I shouldn't be doing. So, if I didn't talk about sex, I reaffirmed to Trent that I believed it was wrong, that it needs to be hidden and not discussed. This further cemented the habit of not talking about sex.

Not talking about sex makes it seem unimportant. The other reason why I didn't want to talk about it was simply because I had no interest, and it wasn't important to me. If I had no interest in books, I wouldn't join a book club to talk about what I wasn't reading.

Because I didn't talk about sex, it sent a message to Trent that that part of our marriage was unimportant to me. That I could take it or leave it. Considering sex is an integral part of marriage, I also sent the message that my marriage itself was unimportant to me.

That's when in 2013, I contemplated a divorce for the first time in my marriage. I was exhausted.

Trent would leave the house before 6 a.m. and would frequently get home after 7 p.m. I resented him for being gone so much. I was closed off both physically and emotionally, and I felt my attraction to him dwindling each month. This feeling was obvious to Trent and made him more depressed each day, as he yearned for connection but also felt like any previous connection was gone from our marriage. It didn't help that he was already feeling a high level of stress from working hard to provide for our family and working longer hours with little to show for it.

Trent felt like he wasn't a good husband or father as he wasn't providing the lifestyle we had become accustomed to living. He connected his worth and value to me to his earning ability. He believed that he was not loved or lovable if he couldn't provide a certain level of income and lifestyle.

One of the greatest tools we ever learned to assist Trent and me in creating our ideal life and marriage, as well as to help me escape my thoughts of divorce, was how to be authentic and vulnerable. Simple as that!

Trent and I go in greater detail about specifics and the process we went through to learn how to communicate which we share in our online *Couples Connection Course*.

Text the word **COUPLES** to **801-505-9750** to learn more about the Couples Connection Course.

Sex is a very personal topic for most people. Discussing it shows vulnerability. In a marriage, it's similarly risky to talk about sex. Talking about sex with your spouse shares a very personal, deep, emotional part of who you are with them. All vulnerability comes with the possibility of being rejected, of being attacked or otherwise hurt. But it's that willingness to be vulnerable and then have that vulnerability accepted that grows emotional intimacy. When you share these embarrassing ideals, beliefs, feelings, hopes, and fears, it opens the door to further intimacy in all areas. Marriage isn't split into discrete parts. Marriage is holistic. Every part impacts all the others.

As a man, Trent wanted so much to maintain the "hero" status in our marriage. He wanted to appear as a man without flaws, not having anything wrong with him that would reveal weaknesses for fear that I wouldn't love him if I knew all the things he dealt with.

I, on the other hand, just didn't want to know that my husband had weaknesses, and I feared what he would think of me if he knew of my struggles. Because of these insecurities, we resisted being authentic.

At first, being authentic can add a large amount of strain to a relationship, but on the other end, if the couple can work through it, there comes a dramatic increase in connection. Together, vulnerability and authenticity can strengthen relationships.

Authenticity is existing without hiding behind a mask. It means allowing total honesty, as is, to show the original and raw you. Authenticity is the gift of heartfelt honesty and committing to expressing your thoughts openly in the moment--and allowing others to do the same. Authenticity asks us to dig a little deeper into who we are and let go of anything that's in the way of being our true selves. It gives the incredible (although scary at first) gift of vulnerability.

Living unauthentically is inherently stressful. It's not natural for us, it takes great effort, and it goes against who we are at the deepest level of our being. When we're living a lie, we need to constantly maintain that lie, cover our bases, and make sure no one discovers who we really are. I'm calling that stressful.

Authenticity is life changing and it's a powerful metabolizer that sets us on our truest course and keeps us real in our relationships. It allows us to be exactly what we are—human. It removes the pretense and "faking it" that we're often taught in order to get by in this world. Authenticity removes the stress of having to be something we are not.

So, the moral of the story here is that if you want to be at your best in your marriage, then you need to be at your personal best. Authenticity is a requirement for a life well-lived and a body that's well nourished.

Are you willing to be honest?

Are you willing to start speaking the truth in your life?

Are you willing to be who you really are?

Are you ready to stop living with so many things holding you back, and speak what's on your mind?

Are you ready to stop pretending, and take the risk to be your most authentic self?

WHAT CHANGED MY PERCEPTION

1. WORK ON YOU, NOT YOUR SPOUSE

If you're in a relationship, are you happy, satisfied, and well taken care of sexually?

If your response is a quick "yes" then get ready to discover many new ways to enhance your relationship. If you hesitated or said "no," then you need to acknowledge the truth about your situation and consider what you could change. We tend to jump too fast into "save" or "fix" mode, when really what we need is to get back on track with ourselves.

That was a huge discovery for me in 2013. I wanted to fix Trent. I didn't think I had anything to work on until someone called me out on how I affected our marriage and our lack of sexual connection. That made me take a hard and deeper look at the problems I was having.

By taking ownership of my current situation, and how I contributed to our relationship being rocky, I allowed myself to feel more in control of improving our marriage. Personal responsibility and ownership on my part in our relationship gave me more agency and helped me see ways in which I could change.

A few of the things I chose to control were working on my self confidence. Self confidence leads to confidence in the bedroom too. By working out daily, taking time to invest in learning and reading about intimacy, I became more empowered and felt worthy of love and sexual connection. It wasn't a matter of having the perfect body, but a matter of self confidence and realizing that I can love myself right where I am in my pursuit of something better.

By wondering how I contributed to our marriage getting so close to divorce, I was empowered with choice, understanding, and control. Here's an honest question: "how have I contributed to our relationship being what it is today, and how can I make it better?"

2. YOU NEVER WILL FULLY CONNECT UNTIL YOU ALLOW FULL AUTHENTICITY AND (OFTEN PAINFUL) VULNERABILITY TO EXIST

In order for you to get to this raw level of vulnerability in your marriage, it requires you both to work toward a deep level of unconditional self-love and approval. You must be okay with your dark side as well as your light side. You must accept your weaknesses and embrace the knowledge that neither you nor your spouse is perfect.

This requires you to be non-judgmental and to see your spouse through God's eyes and recognize that you are both broken in some way and must fully rely on the atonement of our Savior to be made whole. Neither one of you is better than the other; we are equal in that way.

The truth is, the only way to create the deepest level of connection with your spouse is to stop pretending to have it all together. Since Trent was able to drop the mask and I know the real, imperfect man that he is, he has become so much more attractive to me. I see it as a strength for him to open his heart and expose himself in his truest form, trusting me fully to not hurt him. When I became more vulnerable, Trent also noticed an increased attraction for me. He said it added to my "sexy confidence," and he felt more connected to me than at any time in our marriage.

I know it can be scary, but I promise it's worth it. This changed everything for us.

In relationships, when we are not willing to share what we are feeling and thinking, we are not able to connect at the deepest level.

Our marriage has continued to grow and blossom. I can't express the level of love and connection that we've created as we went through several more months of authentic and often painful conversations to get to know and discover each other all over again after years of marriage. It truly feels like we have had a new marriage and a new bond that is stronger than what I had ever imagined was possible.

3. BE HONEST: IT'S TIME TO DISCUSS SEX AND OPENLY AIR OUT ISSUES

When you talk about something that is eating away at you, you get clarity about where the other person is, and you can let things go, choosing instead to focus on what really matters. Talking about issues in relationships can reboot or help build confidence, because you know where you stand with your spouse.

When you remain silent about your difficulties, particularly sexual ones, you stay in a place of shame or insecurity because you have no feedback or information to reframe the stories in your head and help you improve the situation. This can be death to a relationship. I know, because as a sexual health educator, I talk to people who tell me things they don't even tell their spouses—simply because they don't know how to talk about these things. If you know what the problem or issue is, you can work on it.

Learning to have adult sexual conversations is a total confidence builder.

4. DESCRIBE TO YOUR SPOUSE HOW SEX FEELS, WHAT YOU WANT THEM TO DO, AND WHAT YOU'RE ENJOYING

If you both communicate, this can also stop spectatoring. Much of the cause of spectatoring is not knowing things. Not knowing if your spouse is enjoying what you are doing, not knowing if they want to change positions, etc. Having them communicate how they are feeling and enjoying the experience helps you not to worry about it as much. Likewise, you communicating with them helps them not to worry.

5. OPEN OUR MINDS TO OPEN OUR LEGS

When a woman's heart opens and she feels emotionally close, she will open up sexually. If you suddenly look like a jerk, you are immediately going to shut her down.

Most men and women may find that if a man has a good-looking woman, but she is acting like a jerk, she is still good looking to the man and he still may want to have sex with her. If a woman has a good-looking man and he says the wrong thing, he immediately looks like a dog and she is not attracted to him.

Men have to talk about the things she is interested in and what he is interested in. He needs to focus on her sensing organs and intellect. Smell good, touch her in safe ways.

Compliment her, share an interest in her and what she is saying. A small, sincere compliment is much better than a generic or fake compliment to get her to have sex.

6. TALKING ABOUT SEX IMPROVES SEX

Talking about sex improves sex itself. If you can't talk about sex, then you can't address any issues that might occur during sex. You can't express anything but the most basic desires. You can't talk about your struggles, what you want to do, what's working and what isn't. In short, you can't work to make sex any better.

And why wouldn't you want sex to be better? I mean, most of us aren't masters of sex right out of the gate. Probably none of us. I know I'm still not; I still have a lot to learn. But sex keeps getting better. I keep finding out new tricks, which I do my best to share with you. We still have plenty of struggles and opportunities to get better, which I also try to share so that you can feel you aren't alone. I share these on my private Facebook group, Sexual Health with Sarah.

7. TALKING ABOUT SEX INCREASES THE FREQUENCY OF SEX

On average, couples that don't talk about sex have sex about once every 2 weeks. Having even one conversation about sex a year nearly doubled the frequency.

But if you want substantial changes, the numbers indicate that conversations once a month correlate with sex almost twice a week. Weekly conversations jump to slightly more than twice a week. But those talking about sex daily on average have sex 3-4 times per week.

> If you want more sex, talk about it. If you don't want more sex, talk about it and *why*.

The bonus is if you're reading content as well as talking about sex, your desire increases because it's on the forefront of your brain most of the time. I know this from personal experience these past two years, it works.

And the truth is, there is no good reason not to talk about sex. It shouldn't be taboo. It should be as comfortable to talk about as talking about your feelings, your dreams, your hopes and fears. And I know, all those things can be uncomfortable, but they're only uncomfortable because you don't do it often.

8. JUST BECAUSE A MAN KNOWS WHAT TO DO WITH A WOMAN WHEN SHE IS HORIZONTAL, DOESN'T MEAN HE KNOWS WHAT TO DO WITH HER VERTICALLY

Husbands need to ease their wives into a conversation to talk about what she wants in the bedroom. It should be done in a way or place where she can change the subject and both can step away from the conversation if needed. Vertical, clothed, and outside the bedroom. Doing it horizontal or when alone is too vulnerable of a time to talk about sex for many women.

9. WHEN WAS THE LAST TIME..

We might test ourselves by asking a few questions. With a little adaptation, these questions can apply to most of us, whether we are married or single, whatever our home situation might be.

- When was the last time I sincerely praised my companion, either alone or in the presence of our children?

- When was the last time I thanked, expressed love for, or earnestly pleaded in faith for him or her in prayer?

- When was the last time I stopped myself from saying something I knew could be hurtful?

- When was the last time I apologized and humbly asked for forgiveness—without adding the words "but if only you had" or "but if only you hadn't"?

- When was the last time I chose to be happy rather than demanding to be "right"?

Now, if any of these questions lead you to squirm or feel a tinge of guilt just as I did when I first read them from a talk titled, *We'll Ascend Together*, by Linda Burton, learn this:

> *"Guilt is to our spirit what pain is to our body—a warning of danger and a protection from additional damage."*
>
> --David Bednar

Use that guilt (recognition that you did something wrong) to move you to action, not to feel shame.

10. REFER TO STEP 5, AFTERGLOW, IN THE FEMALE SEXUAL RESPONSE CYCLE IN CHAPTER EIGHT

Not talking about this topic of sex will numb you. When we can set aside time to really open and connect emotionally about our wants and concerns about sex then we will see progress. We need to start asking the questions then changing our questions to change our sex life.

CHAPTER FIFTEEN

JUST GET DONE
WITH IT ALREADY

Let me know if this sounds familiar. Occasionally, I've tried to take Trent with me to do some casual clothes shopping. I thought it would be fun to spend some quality time together and just shop. We would get to the mall, wander around and go into a store or two (just to browse of course, not looking for anything in particular), and this is how our interaction would usually play out at each store.

First, we would enter a store. Then, within a few minutes of entering the store, Trent begins asking, "are you done yet?"

Trent obviously has different expectations and didn't enjoy the process of being together and just shopping. When he goes clothes shopping, he enters the store and usually has already decided what he is looking for and knows what he wants. He heads straight to it, maybe getting distracted momentarily by some shoes or hats, but only briefly. He finds the section with the shirt, or pants, or shorts, or suit, or whatever he is looking for. He grabs the size and color, walks to the register, checks out, and is ready to head home within minutes of entering the store. He doesn't appreciate the joy of just shopping; he doesn't enjoy the process, the exploring, and finding something new and unexpected. He rushes through all of that. What a shame.

Know what is also a shame? When I was in the middle of my, "sex is just for my husband" days, I often approached our sex time with this same attitude of, "are you done yet?"

Almost without fail, by about ten minutes into our love-making session (looking back, I don't know if I'd call it that as it was more like a "marital-obligation session"), I would start making these exasperated sighs of frustration as if to say, "just finish already so we can get this over with." Like most men, Trent doesn't mind a quickie every once in a while, but I didn't realize that my sighs that were expressing, "are you done yet?" were not making things enjoyable or even worthwhile for Trent. In fact, they made him feel unwanted and unloved.

Over time, I realized that what Trent was wanting--but didn't know how to ask me--was an experience similar to a good shopping experience! We obviously had different expectations. He didn't want to feel rushed. He wanted to explore and just enjoy being with me. He wanted to explore my body and my pleasure. He wanted to find something new and unexpected.

Together. Instead, I wanted to rush him to the register and get on with life.

Many men fear their egos will be damaged if they don't know what they are doing. They won't admit they can learn something. However, many women fake it to protect their man's ego and avoid the feeling of making him feel like a failure. They may also fake it to get it over with. I'm a pretty good actor when it comes to faking an orgasm. Anyone else? Women are faking orgasms because they think a penis should get them to orgasm and they want the guy involved to think his penis has these powers. But it doesn't. No penis does.

Men, like women, want connection. They just want it in different ways than women. Men don't just want a hole to stick their penis in (sorry for the crude visual, but I want this to be crystal clear). Men want to engage in *lovemaking* with you. Not just sex. A true, loving man wants all of you. Your heart, your mind, your passion, your attention, your desire, and your body. Men don't get connection from women by just using our bodies to reach orgasm. They may not know how to express it, but they want more than just sex.

Now, we both choose to enjoy time with each other and not rush the experience, whether it is shopping or sex.

WHAT CHANGED MY PERCEPTION

1. HAVE OPEN, HONEST, AND JUDGEMENT-FREE CONVERSATIONS ABOUT WHAT YOU'RE LEARNING

Trent and I began to have many more open and honest, judgement-free conversations about our sex. At first, I was uncomfortable, and would try to change the subject, rush off to do chores, or take care of the kids. I did all that I could to avoid talking about sex.

However, once I felt I had permission to learn about sex from my friend Suzanne, I began my journey of learning about my body and what was possible in our marital sex. This education allowed me to feel more and more comfortable talking about sex and not feeling overwhelmed or completely ignorant.

2. I WANTED TO UNDERSTAND HIM

When we were able to finally both share--when we both had confidence that we could remain in a state of curiosity, wanting to understand each other, and wanting to help each other feel whole and satisfied-- we could finally talk about what I was doing that was creating separation instead of connecting during sex.

In Chapter Three I mentioned a book called *For Women Only*; I highly recommend this read if you truly want to understand a man. The thought, "just get it done already," ran through my mind when I began to be frustrated with Trent during sex because he was taking too long. But this book taught me about the man's view and the importance of feeling wanted. I wanted to seek to understand Trent. I finally asked, and he was able to share with me specific ideas in which I can show him that he feels wanted. These are some things I do to show him that I want him and care for him:

- Running my fingers through his hair as we sit next to each other.

- Being the one to approach him and hold his hand or cuddle up next to him.

- Whispering something to him that I know is a turn on.

- Coming up to him when he gets home and giving him a passionate, loving 6 second kiss.

- Initiating sex from time to time (as opposed to him always being the initiator. Trust me, if you are the responder and he is the pursuer in your relationship, try flipping this, and see how loved and appreciated he feels).

3. WE LEARNED ABOUT THE CYCLE THAT WE WOMEN GO THROUGH TO REACH AROUSAL, DESIRE AND ORGASM

It still took us a while to finally figure out what I really needed to be prepared for sex so that both our needs were being met. Because men and women are so different in the way we are stimulated and prepare for sex, all men and women *need* to understand how women's minds and bodies work when it comes to sex, arousal, desire, and orgasm. Be sure to refer Chapter Eight, *"The Female Sexual Response Cycle"*.

CHAPTER SIXTEEN

I HATE HAVING TO SCHEDULE SEX

I love schedules. I love to be organized and to know hour by hour what my plans are. I began to put sex in my schedule because I knew it was important to Trent and I knew he would appreciate me putting him into my schedule.

Over time I started to notice how distant I began to feel from him and the pressure to check that box off my list. Just knowing that sex was in my calendar created a lot of anxiety and my mind began to play tricks on me. I would allow myself to find other activities to override the sex on my schedule.

For some women maybe scheduling sex works for them but I would have you consider how present you are when you are together. I felt an added stress to perform even more because it was on the schedule and he was expecting me to be all in.

Science says there is a direct correlation between having sex at least once a week and relationship happiness. Still, the idea of scheduling sex at a specific time and date may make you feel like you do when you are taking your car in for its scheduled maintenance.

Clinical psychologist Dr. Samantha Rodman has a perspective-shifting way of presenting the idea. Don't get overly specific, she suggests:

"Knowing 'Friday is the day for sex even if I'm exhausted and the kids were up all night or I have a headache it doesn't work for me or for many people. Instead, try something like, 'If I wake up before you and the kids on any given weekday, I will initiate sex with you' or 'Any nap time that the kids are all asleep at once is game time' or 'Weekends are our time.' Making the window wider may actually increase the number of times you have sex because it's not so much pressure."

WHAT CHANGED MY PERCEPTION

1. MAKE SEX A PRIORITY

I have made sex a priority in my marriage this past two years, and so should you.

Consider this:

I felt that all I did all day was meet other people's needs. Whether it was caring for my children, working around the house or in my business, by the end of the day I wanted to be done need-meeting. I wanted to sit in my swinging Guatemala chair and just read a book.

But God prompted me with:

> **"Are the 'needs' you meet for your husband the needs he wants met?"**

If I didn't have a plan for dinner but food was in the fridge, he didn't complain. If the kitchen floor needed mopping, he didn't say a word. And if he didn't have any underwear to wear, he simply threw them in the washer himself.

I soon realized I regularly said "no" to the one thing he asked of me; to physically and emotionally connect. I sure wasn't making myself available to my husband by militantly adhering to *my* plan for the day.

Would the world end if I didn't get that kitchen drawer organized or wash my car? I'd been so focused on what I wanted to get done and what my children needed, I'd cut my husband out of the picture.

I soon realized that I too needed to meet my own sexual needs. I began to see that making sex a priority for me did improve my day-to-day life because I was less crabby and snappy at my family. I saw changes in me after I had sex where I felt more creative and productive in my work. I noticed Trent appreciating and serving me more because we were both making sex a priority in our marriage.

2. HAVE BETTER SEX BY STARTING EARLIER

So, how are you going to change your habits based on this information? Could you choose one or two nights a week where you decide to have sex earlier in the evening? Maybe you could have your fun before finishing your chores. Have you considered morning time, or--if possible--a lunch break?

After all, you're an adult; it doesn't always have to be work before play. Try it out and see if it improves your sex life. Or just skip the chores one night. It might be worth it.

3. YOU DON'T HAVE TO FALL ASLEEP AFTER SEX

I know, I'm mostly talking to the husbands here, but there are some women who get pretty sleepy after sex as well.

There's nothing better than slipping into a post-orgasm coma after an enthusiastic round of sex. I get that. But, if it's at the expense of having really good sex, is it really worth it?

I mean, if the choice is to have great sex while you still have lots of energy, or mediocre sex because you're already exhausted and then be able to fall asleep immediately afterward, which would you choose?

So, have sex earlier and then, if need be, take a shower to wake yourself up a bit so you can do all the things you would have done before sex.

4. AS AN ADULT, GOING TO BED EARLY ISN'T A PUNISHMENT

I don't know about your household, but at mine, bedtime always seems to come as a surprise to my kids, as if they don't have one every single day. Wrangling five kids into bed (usually in 2-3 shifts due to age differences) is a chore and a half.

I think as adults, we sometimes have the idea that going to bed early is still a punishment for something. We don't want to go to bed early, because, well, we're adults now! We don't have to.

From my perspective though, you're an adult. You *get* to go to bed early. I mean, let's face it, we're not talking about going to bed to sleep. We're talking about going to bed to have fun and reconnect. Don't treat it like a punishment, but rather a reward.

5. DON'T LET YOUR KIDS BE YOUR EXCUSE

I used this excuse *all the time* and tend to catch myself at times still using it. Yes, their noises can distract you, but over time, your mind will begin to tune them out. Tuning out the noise is a skill, and the more you do it, the easier it will get. If you want connection while the kids are home, you will make a creative effort to do so.

Part of the challenge is you may have the belief that it's wrong to have your kids hear you having sex. Or you may fear that if your kids are home and awake, they could walk in on you. Or if they start fighting, you might feel your mommy senses go crazy as you feel the need to intervene.

I know all of these fears and concerns all too well. I lived with all those excuses of why sex could only happen when no kids were awake or no kids were home.

Below are some things I've learned that have helped me overcome the issues with worrying about the kids fighting, our kids hearing us have sex, or the general noises they make while we are trying to focus.

My kids may fight, but they always figure it out on their own if I'm busy with Trent. It's good for your kids to work things out on their own. If I have chosen to be intimate with Trent and I can hear the kids start fighting or arguing, I redirect my mind and remind myself "they aren't going to kill each other; they can figure it out on their own."

This technique of allowing your children to fight and work it out actually comes from a few different parenting courses I've taken. As parents, we don't need to always intervene. Sometimes we do, but most of the time we don't. Our children learn important conflict resolution skills when we aren't always interfering.

What about those random noises kids make, reminding you they are just down the hall? One thing that has helped me is to put AirPods in and put on our "sexy time" playlist to tune out the little noises. I suggest you and your spouse create your own playlist if you don't already have one.

If you'd like to hear my "sexy time" playlist, text the word **RESOURCES** to 801-505-9750.

Finally, is it okay for your children to know that you are having sex? While we don't go out of our way to announce it, we have been having age-appropriate discussions with each of our children since they were 8 years old, so they know that we are sexually active. We don't try to make it known, but we also aren't ashamed if they happen to hear some noise coming from our room. We want our children to know that sex in marriage is great and model for them that they should frequently connect with their spouses when they get married.

6. BE CREATIVE & SPONTANEOUS

Two things we have found that make sex more fun are spontaneity and creativity. Most of us react very positively to these two things when it comes to sex. However, with kids, work, extended family, plus dozens of other things demanding our attention, most couples find themselves in a rut when it comes to these being creative or spontaneous with sex.

Trent and I have loved the book, *101 Nights of Great Sex* by Laura Corn for bringing some creativity to our lovemaking. In it are different ideas for men and women to initiate sex. You tear out the page and use the instructions to create a fun time with your spouse. This isn't a "let's pull out the book right before sex" type of thing. They often require a little thought and preparation hours or days before.

One night, Trent used some of the suggestions from one of the ideas from the *101 Nights of Great Sex* book. He surprised me with dinner out in Park City, a fun ski town 45 min away from our home. After dinner he sent me into the grocery store as the first step to a scavenger hunt to grab some items on his shopping list (strawberries and whipped cream) while unbeknownst to me he grabbed a bag he had backed from our trunk and took an Uber to a hotel nearby. He got some music and candles going. I came out of the grocery store to find him gone and followed the next instructions to go to the address in the GPS. I parked at the hotel, went to the front desk as instructed, and got a room key. The rest of the story is private, but we had a great night and a fun morning the next day, too.

There is something about a surprise overnight trip when your husband plans out everything including making sure the kids are taken care of that adds to enthusiasm and keeps the spark you first ignited when you married each other going. Creativity doesn't have to go to this length, but a few times a year, this sort of thing is well-justified to keep your flame burning.

Lastly, how do you enjoy more spontaneity? It really comes down to agreeing to create novelty when it's done at a time you least expect it and when the stars align.

I'm not telling you that you should or should not schedule sex, but I am suggesting to be more spontaneous and creative about how it happens. Maybe a better goal would be how many times you'd like to have sex per week or per month instead of setting specific times in your schedule.

CHAPTER SEVENTEEN

SEX IS JUST PHYSICAL

Friday night sex typically happens after our date night. It's not guaranteed, but it's something we look forward to.

One Friday night, it didn't happen though. It could have. It almost did. The kids were all asleep, the conditions were perfect. We were naked in bed, almost ready to go. Except I wasn't there. I mean, I was physically there, but mentally, I wasn't. I wanted to be and had spent the day trying to gear up for sex.

But I had too much stuff going on in my head that needed to be addressed.

So, what do you do in these situations?

We could have had sex. By that, I mean we could have pushed through, gotten me to switch gears and make the best of it, and just had mediocre sex.

Instead, we talked for the next two hours. Trent probably wouldn't say talking and listening for two hours felt better than sex, because that would be a lie. It wasn't a fun time. There were a lot of tears and hugs and silence. It wasn't fun, but it was good, *really* good emotionally. Maybe you can relate to the feeling.

And you know what? Not long ago, Trent would have missed it. He probably would have pushed for mediocre sex because that's what he was focused on (getting more sex, whenever possible). He wouldn't have recognized the opportunity to connect with me at a deeper level when I needed it. You know what came from that talk? A few amazing love-making sessions that were much better than the mediocre sex that could have happened.

As much as we now both enjoy sex, sex is ultimately a deep expression of intimacy. It's not intimacy itself. Sex can build intimacy and intimacy can lead to great sex, but don't confuse the two. Just because you're having sex, doesn't mean you're experiencing intimacy.

When we truly can be honest and open up to our spouse, to share our not-so-pretty side, and still feel loved, that is where true connection and intimacy in sex begins. When Trent sees all of me, even my dark side (my weaknesses, negative thoughts, and temptations that I deal with), and still loves me and wants to have sex with me, nothing feels so real and so connected.

Sex is good, but intimate sex is way better. There is something special about knowing someone that deeply and being known intimately. When you begin to open up or your spouse begins to open up, if it is a new experience, I want to warn you that it isn't easy. It's uncomfortable and it can hurt to go through it. But it is worth it. Fully opening up or fully knowing someone won't happen all at once, but over dozens and dozens of conversations, you can begin to share more and more of you and understand more and more of your spouse.

This is the truth. Trent and I didn't have deep, connected, intimate sex until he was finally willing to trust me enough to share his dark side; all his weaknesses, his worries, his stresses, his concerns, and his thoughts. He stopped trying to pretend that everything was good and that he had it all under control. This opened the door for me to share my dark side. My fears, my weaknesses, and my frustrations.

When you are willing and able to finally show yourself fully to your spouse, and they to you, that is when sex and intimacy can be life-changing and marriage-binding. Sure, you could have passionate sex with a stranger, but when it is over, you will be left empty. You will never have intimate, amazing sex that fills your soul and binds you to another person until you have fully revealed yourself and your spouse has finally been able to do the same.

I think most of us couldn't understand this early on in our marriages. You may not even be able to see it now. I'm sure some of you are thinking, "I haven't shared a lot of stuff that I struggle with and that I have to battle, but our sex is still great." All I will say to that is until you have tried being truly vulnerable and authentic, you won't know how much deeper your relationship could be and how much better and more connected you could feel.

Sure, our relationship isn't perfect, and we've had some very hard, tear-filled conversations with ugly crying, but our intimacy and trust has been built on those conversations. Out of the hard conversations, we've found stronger foundations to our marriage. Out of those deep, painful conversations (combined with love and desire to support each other) have come our trust and confidence in each other.

I find Trent to be sexiest when he is willing to open up and reveal his imperfect self to me. In those moments, I see him as a humble, loving husband with such deep love for me that he is willing to let me in to see and hear what no one else has probably seen or heard before.

Men, if you are reading this, it's probably because your wife said, "you should read this part," and that means something. It means that she wants you. All of you. Not just the tough, manly man; she wants the weak side of you that is working through things, that struggles with things, that needs her love and support to work through them. She also wants you to hear her and love her just as she is, with all her imperfections. Listen from a place of love and curiosity as you try to understand and help each other. Life is hard enough;

why go through all the stress and pressures alone when you have a loving spouse who wants to work through all the good and the bad together?

Here is the good news: intimacy leads to more and better sex. But you must be willing to risk not having sex sometimes in order to get there. You might forego having sex a few times as deep, important conversations need to happen. They might bring up some painful stuff, but on the other side is some of the best, intimate sex you can imagine.

I want you to reach for something better than normal, every-day sex. If you focus too much on just having sex, you might miss out on creating intimacy and strength in your marriage. So, in order to get what you want (more and/or better sex), be willing to have long, hard conversations.

WHAT CHANGED MY PERCEPTION

1. SEX IS THE GLUE THAT HOLDS THE MARRIAGE TOGETHER

I heard this analogy about a cake and sex. If you think sex is the icing on the cake of marriage, then you're baking that cake without any eggs and it's going to fall apart.

For those of you who are bakers (which I am not), you know what eggs do in a recipe. Eggs are the glue. They're the bonding ingredient. They hold the cake together. You know what happens when you make a cake without eggs? It falls to pieces.

You know what happens to marriages that don't have healthy sex lives? Yeah, they fall to pieces, too. You can have a cake without icing. It's still a cake. No one will argue that it's not a cake. It may not be a fancy cake, but it's still clearly a cake. But a cake without eggs, well, it falls apart.

Sex is not icing. It's not optional, and it's certainly *not* decoration.

For the first 16 years of our marriage, I really liked my decoration on my cake. But it led me to notice how far I was drifting away from Trent. Sex is not frivolous. It is the glue that holds our relationships together. It's what nurtures our intimacy.

When marriages have unhealthy, stressed, or unengaged sex lives, you see marriages start to unravel. It starts coming out in how we communicate. How we look at each other. How we talk about each other. Without sex, the marriage starts to crumble because relationships naturally drift apart. People never drift closer together. Without that glue, it's hard to tolerate another sinful human being so close to you in your everyday life.

But with that bonding ingredient in marriage--what a difference. It's not hard to tolerate them. It's a joy. Sex not only holds the relationship together, but it makes it a marriage.

Sex is not icing on the cake; it's the eggs in the cake!

I'm grateful that I chose to put my eggs in that cake this past year and bond Trent and me in ways I didn't see as possible. Our marriage has been the best it's ever been, even with our ups and downs, because we choose each day to make the eggs work!

2. MARITAL INTIMACY IS A SACRED, GOD-GIVEN EXPRESSION OF LOVE

If you were to believe that marital intimacy can be a kind of sacred God-given expression--a time which can draw you and your spouse closer together and to the Lord--how would you want to prepare differently?

You are preparing for marital intimacy with the thoughts you have about men and women, love and marriage--every day of your life.

If you believe Lucifer's lies about sexual relationships, you will never experience what God intended for a husband and wife to share.

Anything that helps married couples connect at a deeply intimate level is good. Become a student. Get the truth before you get naked. That's what God wants.

3. INTO-ME-SEE IS THE NEW INTIMACY

Since marriage used to be, largely, an economic enterprise, Esther Perel, Psychotherapist and Author of *Mating in Captivity,* said intimacy had to do with sharing a life together: *"you milked the cows, watered the land, and raised the children."* Now it's a very different thing.

"Today when I talk about intimacy, I talk about it as 'into-me-see,'" Perel said. "What I bring to you isn't my dowry or commercial assets. I bring to you my inner life. My wishes, my feelings, my aspirations, my anxieties. And when I talk to you, I want you to look at me. I want contact, I want connection, I want you to make me feel like I matter. When we see that we can share our most prized, deep assets like our feelings, worries, aspirations, dreams, and anxieties then Into-me-see happens. I will open myself up to you to come in and as you come in you will validate me, you will reflect me, and you will momentarily help me transcend my existential aloneness."

4. A MAN'S CONFIDENCE GROWS OUTSIDE THE BEDROOM

I've learned how when I make an effort and come to him with love and a desire to have sex, he turns into an even more powerful and confident man. He serves me more; he has more capacity to love and spend time with our children. His drive, his motivation, his ability to do hard things, they all increase. He becomes a different man when he feels loved, appreciated and wanted by me.

On the flip side, when I draw away from him sexually, put him off and make him feel bad for wanting to connect with me sexually, he feels less driven, less appreciated, and less loved. He feels emasculated. He withdraws from me emotionally and feels unsure about our relationship.

5. ART OF SEDUCTION

The biological need to have sex for women drops off the longer they are married. This is why men sometimes feel like they were tricked ("she was into it when we first got married").

Men often stop seducing their wives shortly after being married. This leads to his wife having less and less desire.

If you get lazy and turn sex into a seven-minute process on Wednesday nights, don't expect her to be interested and want it. You can't be a lousy lover and expect your wife to want more sex.

After I gave myself permission to read recreationally to figure out how my body worked, my mind began to go from a place of judgement to curiosity. It began to fuel my imagination, and it energized my soul to become the lover I desired to be when I first got married.

The art of seduction is to ask yourself what you should do to tease your lover. Often, it's just a hint, the tiniest little clue left lying about early in the week to remind them that you have a surprise in store for them. I'm not that creative to come up with these clever creative scenes in my head. It takes practice and forethought, so use the book I mentioned before called *101 Nights of Great Sex* to help you.

Feel free to change and tweak a few of the ideas in the book to your level of comfort, but over time you'll begin to see a shift in your attitude towards these ideas of seduction and anticipate when you will practice the next one.

No matter how much or little time you have, you can still make this work. Each of us was created to give each other exactly what we're looking for. We want to know what turns on our spouses. We want them to know what turns us on. We'd like more variety, more foreplay, more surprises, more interest, and once in a while, somebody else should do all the work.

You might learn to love something new; don't be ashamed, especially if the two of you have agreed! Be patient with your spouse. You'll want to get to the point where the important thing is to make your spouse's pleasure top priority at least once a week. What great memories you will make together to strengthen your intimate relationship.

CHAPTER EIGHTEEN

PAST TRAUMA HAS MADE IT SO THAT I CAN'T ENJOY SEX

This is a sensitive subject and I am not going to claim for one minute to be the expert or the best resource on dealing with sexual trauma. I will refer to additional resources if you want to dive deeper into the subject of overcoming sexual trauma. This topic comes up far too often when I am meeting with women one-on-one. This is a big factor in why many women struggle with sex and intimacy. I will say with confidence that it is difficult, but very possible for most women to overcome many of the effects of sexual abuse and trauma, through professional help, to have a loving, connected relationship with their spouse.

Sex. This amazing, bonding experience that couples share to express love and devotion has been defiled and mocked and made disgusting and vile for many women because it was forced on them in one way or another, usually as a child or young adult. What for many has been a very sacred, connecting, pleasurable, and unifying thing is seen as horrifying, painful, and a major trigger for many of those affected by sexual abuse. Unfortunately, 1 in 4 girls will be sexually abused before they turn 18 and 90% of them will know their perpetrator as cited by The Younique Foundation. The Younique Foundation was created for the purpose of helping women who are survivors of childhood sexual abuse.

If you have been a victim of sexual abuse or experienced sexual trauma, I want to first express that I am deeply pained by any experience I hear, and I'm so sorry this happened to you. You must believe and know that it's not your fault. You didn't do anything to deserve this, and this should not have happened to you. You are not alone.

Whether it be rape or sexual abuse by a family member, family friend, neighbor, trusted person of authority, or a complete stranger, sexual abuse is rampant across the world. The reality is these numbers of abuse are actually probably lower and underreported. These traumatic experiences lead to some major hurdles and concerns when it comes to connecting with a spouse through sexual intimacy.

Recently I attended a conference and was able to listen to Sarah Klein, one of many gymnasts who was sexually abused by Dr. Larry Nassar. Larry is a convicted American serial child molester, who was a former USA Gymnastics national team doctor and osteopathic physician at Michigan State University.

She shared her experience about the sexual abuse that started when she was eight years old and lasted for 17 years. Sarah shared, *"some of the mental and emotional effects of sexual trauma can be guilt, shame, anger, low self-esteem, dissociation with your body, depression, inability to trust or be touched, and a fear of intimacy. You may experience a diminished connection to your body and mind. You no longer see your body as a source of pleasure and may also be numbed so you don't experience pain."*

Some of the effects on a woman's body sexually are:

- Avoiding sex in general and feeling distant and alienated.

- Feeling a lack of desire even when you want to have sex.

- Feeling out of control with your sexuality and/or being over sexualized.

- Feeling uncomfortable or fearful, angry, and even disgusted by touch, especially by strangers.

- Feeling genital pain.

- Flashbacks in response to certain words, touches and/or even scenarios.

Listen to your body. What touch feels good, bad, or triggering? Have a frank conversation with your spouse about this.

These effects ripple not only through your family, but also your neighborhoods and workplaces. So take care of yourself where you can, and know that it is entirely normal to have bad days.

WHAT CHANGED MY PERCEPTION

1. KNOWING HOW TO SUPPORT A SURVIVOR OF SEXUAL ABUSE

Avoid judgement--don't take on the role of therapist or co-dependent. That's the worst thing you can do for them. Be that safe and non-judgmental friend or sister and just listen intently.

Check in with them periodically--once they've disclosed to you, don't just drop them and don't ever talk about it again. Be there for them to check in and let them know you care and are their biggest supporter.

2. KNOW THE RESOURCES

The following self-help books and online resources are excellent to guide you through this trauma you've experienced:

Maltz, Wendy. *The Sexual Healing Journey: A Guide for Survivors of Sexual Abuse*

Davis, Laura. T*he Courage to Heal: A Guide to Women Survivors of Child Sexual Abuse*

Bastian, Sariah*. Beyond Breath* and/or her online Prana course at sariahbastian.com

rainn.org / 800-656-HOPE / youniquefoundation.org

3. HEALING IS A PROCESS

Nobody ever arrives. You may look like you have it put together, but it's a process. Once you begin to use your voice and share your story, then others will feel empowered to share theirs too. You heal when you speak the truth as well as supporting one another. We've *all* had adversity, and life is messy. Healing is about voice and hope.

4. DON'T HIDE, DON'T LIVE IN SHAME, AND TALK ABOUT TOUGH ISSUES

That's the only way we will affect change. Have the courage to speak up. Every single heart matters, has worth, has value and has a story. Your story matters. We each have a different and unique story that can affect someone and be an "aha" for them to make change. When you can, pay it forward.

5. HOW DO WE CHANGE THE CULTURE AND THE MOMENTUM

We do it together as an army of women! We build each other up. Women will raise other women up. Keep showing up and celebrating one another. That is where the magic happens and that is *hope*!

Let us be at the front lines of helping women own their bodies and their voices. We are in many instances the reason someone might have the courage to use their voice.

CHAPTER NINETEEN

HIS INFIDELITY/PORN USE HAS TURNED ME OFF

This can be a very painful topic for some, so I'll attempt to tread lightly while still offering some perspective and ideas on how to work through this if it has affected your marriage. While women can also be unfaithful or use porn, it's more common that women are feeling the pain of their husband's choices to use porn or be unfaithful.

When learning of pornography use or infidelity for the first time, most women say it is as if a switch was flipped and their desire to be with their husband sexually "turned off." After about 12 years of marriage, Trent and I had a frank conversation where he shared that he had been using pornography as an escape from stress and life when things were hard. At that time in our marriage, I knew I wasn't the best wife, but I also had been working on myself the previous six months. It was hard to hear, but I knew that it wasn't *me* that caused this. I was lucky in that I was prepared to hear this and knew my worth as a daughter of God. I knew that his choices didn't make me less valuable. The initial shock was still hard to hear. I cried. I asked, "why me and my marriage?" and felt angry.

Trust me, I get it. It's hard to feel attracted to your spouse when you find out they've been looking at other women and masturbating to pornography. It's even harder if you find out they cheated on you and shared with someone else, the one thing that is supposed to be exclusive and sacred to your marriage relationship. For many women, they feel these violations of trust are too hard to come back from. They feel that they can't see their spouse the same ever again.

While that might be the case for some, I've worked with several women who are able to take those signs that something is broken in their marriage and work with their spouse to fix their marriage, so it is stronger than ever before. This may or may not be possible with your relationship, but I want you to know that there is hope, that through the atonement of Christ, your marriage can be healed if you are *both* willing to work at it.

It is obviously very easy to blame your spouse if they are looking at pornography or have cheated on you. While they are 100% in the wrong for choosing those actions, putting all the blame on them for those actions takes away any power you have to create a different outcome. If you are stuck for too long being the victim and can plan on holding onto negative feelings towards your spouse indefinitely, then you might as well end the marriage. A marriage cannot be healed if we hold on to those feelings for too long and continue to bring up the same mistake over and over and hold it over our spouse's head.

Learning of broken trust in your marriage causes a natural and normal flood of emotions ranging from anger, mourning the loss of what you once had, bitterness, deep sadness, and even depression. These are okay to feel and may last for weeks, months, or sometimes years if the violation of trust is severe. For some, when a violation of trust of this nature is discovered, it is almost like finding out a loved one has passed away.

Now to be clear, I am not advocating consequence-free forgiveness here. However, we also get to identify and own our part of the marriage that allowed our spouse's heart to wander. He may have been a cheater all along and we ignored the signs, but more commonly, we find that something was broken in the relationship that led to the loss of connection and created an opportunity for this to happen.

I want this to be very clear. This is not your fault. You didn't want it or ask for it, but you also can choose to humbly recognize if any of your actions or lack of action in your marriage in some way contributed to your spouse wandering to the point of violating your trust and disregarding your feelings and marriage vows. In rare cases, the wife's trust that was violated had nothing to do whatsoever with the husband viewing pornography or cheating. I say this is rare, because what I am sharing in this chapter has come from hours and hours of very hard conversations. Conversations with divorced men, with married men who've had an affair, men who have struggled with pornography, and with couples about what causes men to turn to pornography or seeking emotional and physical validation that they are wanted and needed from someone outside their marriage.

Now before we dive into why otherwise normal, good, Christian men look at pornography, I want to talk about what most of these men would say they value in their marriage.

If you were to ask 100 good Christian men, *"would you rather feel loved or respected by your wife?"* they would first say both, but when pushed to choose one, most would say respected.

When a man feels respected, he feels like his wife sees his worth, his value, his sacrifices, and his strengths. When a man feels disrespected, he feels worthless, unwanted, emasculated, and not needed. For men, feeling wanted, needed, and respected are the foundation to feeling connected to their spouse. You may feel, and are right in believing, that not all men deserve respect. However, I believe most Christian men who are trying to live good lives deserve respect for many of the things they do for their families, despite their character flaws or weaknesses.

You cannot have respect only for men who are perfect, because they don't exist. You get to identify what parts of your spouse you are grateful for and show them appreciation and respect for those things. He might be a good provider; he might be a good father and spend time with their children. He is probably kind in most circumstances. Focus on the positive instead of the negative, but don't let this focus on the positive be permission to allow abuse in any form.

Pornography use has skyrocketed in the past two decades. Prior to widespread use of internet and now smartphones, access to pornography was limited to one or two cable channels with late night porn. Or the magazine sold at the seedy store in town that most Christian men would not dare venture into, for fear of being seen by someone they know. I doubt most Christian men would dare subscribe to one of those magazines either, for fear their spouse would intercept it in the mail. Prior to probably the 1980s, magazines were likely the only place for most people to access pornography.

This issue for Christian men is a relatively new problem, as access is instant and easily accessible. Within seconds of having an urge to look at pornography, one can access years' worth of unique video content from pornography video streaming websites. No need to go to a public place and risk being seen, or have it delivered in a way where a spouse or someone else might intercept it.

I believe that part of the reason pornography use is so prevalent, even in Christian homes, is the fact that it is such an easy form of escapism to hide and there is so much shame around it. If someone does drugs or consumes an excessive amount of alcohol to escape from reality, those closest to them definitely know. It's too hard to hide either the smell or the side effects. With pornography, it is likely the easiest form of escapism for Christian men to access that is also fairly easy to hide. It is simple to have a quick fix. It makes men (and sometimes women, too) feel like they are in a different world where the person on the screen is wanting or desiring them for this brief moment. Then comes the crash. They feel ashamed and like they have no control over their desires. This re-affirms the belief or thought, "I am not wanted" or "I am not good enough."

No wonder this tool is used by Satan to destroy so many marriages and relationships. The desire to be wanted and needed is never fulfilled in this escape from reality, and the cycle of shame that comes after reinforcing the false belief of not being good enough and not being wanted.

Because God gave mankind not only the power to procreate, but for most men and some women, a high sex drive, it is important to recognize that sex is for pleasure and connection as well as procreation. When we become one by engaging in sex in a way that meets one another's needs, we are creating a tighter bond, a feeling of being wanted and desired by our spouse. In a healthy relationship, feeling wanted and connected diminishes or removes the desire to view pornography or look outside the marriage to feel wanted or desired.

Now, it is not that simple. There are other factors to it, but for many men, finally shedding the mask, sharing what they are struggling with, and feeling understood and connected to their spouse greatly reduces the desire to view pornography. When they are seen by their wife as a son of God, who loves his family, but is struggling as he is trying to navigate emotions and desires and seeking to be respected and wanted, the shame begins to fall away. When shame dissipates or disappears, many men find the desire and urge to view pornography is reduced significantly.

You may have heard the phrase "don't feed the beast." This is a true statement but is often misapplied in marriages where pornography has a hold on one of the spouses. If a spouse views pornography, by denying them sex to try and "tame their sex drive" or simply "punish them," you are actually making it harder for them to overcome the compulsion to view pornography. They feel less wanted, less connected, and less empowered to overcome. Connection and communication, while removing shame, are the most powerful tools to help a man overcome the urge to view pornography.

I don't condone simply giving your spouse as much sex as they want to try and "cure" them. That isn't the solution. I suggest having conversations, which are often difficult, in order to identify the root cause of this chasm in your marriage. You also need to find out if you and your spouse are willing to work on healing. This starts with laying down specific boundaries and ways in which your spouse can begin to regain trust and repair (as much as is possible) the damage.

It is 100% absolutely normal to lack desire to have sex with your husband when you learn of infidelity or pornography use. If this complete lack of desire continues for weeks or months while your spouse is actively working to regain your trust and making progress, you should strongly consider therapy and counseling. There are good therapists, okay therapists, and I have heard stories of bad therapists. However, the marriage has more chance of healing when you can address the root causes of your problems. If that is not possible for you two alone, then I strongly encourage getting outside help to assist you with communicating about the hard things that are not being addressed.

Once you are at the point where you feel trust is being re-established, focusing on creating more fulfilling and connecting sex will actually help your husband to reduce and in some cases almost completely remove the temptation to turn to pornography for escape or release. When a spouse feels wanted, needed, and desired sexually, they often feel sexually satisfied (this usually means more than just checking the "we had sex" box a couple times per month).

If someone has a sweet tooth and consumes way too many unhealthy carbs and you want to help them be healthy, you don't deprive them of all food! That makes it so easy for them to simply reach a breaking point and binge, consuming even more sweets/carbs! What you do is increase the protein and vegetables in their diet and increase their activity, so they are satiated with healthy foods and slowly, the desire for sweets is diminished because they are always full with healthy foods.

Now, while this is not a direct comparison to a compulsion to view pornography, there are many correlating points that are true. When a spouse is viewing pornography and trying to hide, usually (not always) it is because they have low self-esteem because they are not feeling wanted or needed by their spouse (whether from their own choices or not, the result is the same). From my experience, getting angry at the spouse who is viewing pornography and simply denying them sex, they just feel worse (lower self-esteem), and less connected, less wanted, less needed, and are often pushed right to the breaking point and fall back on the escape from reality that pornography has created for them.

Most Christian men that have or have had a problem with pornography will tell you they wish they didn't look at porn and wish they could kill that desire to view pornography completely. It is not something they want at their core. They want to have a healthy sexual relationship with their spouse. They want to feel connected. They want to feel wanted. They want to feel needed. They want to please their spouse sexually. The problem is that neither spouse usually knows how to meet these desires, or they don't go deep enough in their discussions if they talk about sex at all. Wives of men who view pornography often don't want to have sex because of one of the many reasons we've previously discussed in this book. This lack of connection often (but not always) is the thing that is feeding the overwhelming desire to look at pornography, to escape from reality and briefly escape from feeling not good enough, feeling not wanted or needed.

Having said all of that, I do not believe in giving men a free pass or letting them off the hook for their decisions. This is *not* "the wife's problem," and simply having a higher frequency sex isn't the solution. Men do have control over their decisions, and even if they don't feel wanted, needed, or desired by their wife right now, it does not give them permission to indulge in escape and seek after lustful desires. You both get to work on what part you bring to the relationship that either causes disconnect or increases connection. You own your choices and the consequences and your husband gets to own his. Work together in love with a desire to heal and work on your own selves to bring more confidence and connection to your marriage.

I want to offer you this hope: whatever direction your spouse chooses in regard to pornography use or infidelity, you get to choose to work on yourself. Whether your increased confidence and self-esteem from working on yourself brings more connection to your marriage or not, it will prepare you for whatever the future holds. Whether or not your husband chooses something different, you will still benefit from working on you. Own your part in your current relationship and start working on improving the balance in your life to heal your relationship or prepare for the future. Eat healthy, work out, read uplifting and self-improvement books. Connect with God. All these things bring more self-love and confidence. You can only control you.

WHAT CHANGED MY PERCEPTION

1. NOT FOCUSING ON WHEN HE WILL RELAPSE AGAIN

How do I know Trent will never relapse again? I don't. But I know that I've never seen him happier or felt more trust and love in our relationship as we have by being in recovery. If I am always worrying about "what if," it makes it hard to focus on connecting. The more I focus on showing him respect in the areas where I see it is deserved, the more connected we feel and the more connected our sex. With connected sex and a man who feels wanted and respected, I don't have to constantly worry about, "what if he relapses?"

2. I CAN'T FIX THE COMPULSION

How do I know he's not lying to me or viewing pornography? I know because I can feel it in our interactions, and I know that God will confirm to me what's right and the truth of all things. And most of all, I know that Trent is ultimately in charge of his actions and knows he can talk to me without shame when he is feeling tempted; it's also not my job to make sure I keep tabs on him. He gets to determine his happiness in life, and by freeing myself from obsessing over whether he's okay, I can be okay. Most of all, it's not my job to save Trent. I can only control myself and my choices and actions. I just choose to stay connected to him, and he has chosen to stay connected to me.

3. FORGIVENESS IS BRINGING BROKEN PIECES TO GOD AND ALLOWING HIM TO HEAL, COMFORT, RECONCILE AND REDEEM.

A big piece to this hard and complicated puzzle of forgiveness for me personally is resentment. It only hurts me, not the person I'm trying to forgive. It affects my interactions, my health, and my sanity. It's like emotional suicide.

One of the reasons you can't let go of that hurt, get past the hangup, or get over the habit is that when you hold on to unresolved relationships, bitterness takes root in your heart and causes all kinds of trouble.

> *"Forgiveness is the vehicle used for correcting our misperceptions and for helping us let go of fear. Simply stated, to forgive is to let go."*
> --Gerald Jampolsky, Author

Forgiveness is letting go of the hope for a better past.

Are you standing in your own way because your man hurt you?

If you feel stuck in any area of your life, especially with your sex life, it could very well be due to a lack of forgiveness. Maybe you didn't forgive him. Maybe you didn't forgive yourself. It doesn't matter. Holding on to past emotions, memories, or stories is guaranteed to tie up your energy and block your ability to attract what you want. What you have to do now is forgive.

I used to struggle with this one. I was afraid that if I forgave someone, I would not learn the lesson they gave me, and I would be suckered again. But as I looked at that belief, I realized it was just that: a belief. It wasn't real. It wasn't factual. It wasn't true.

4. FORGIVENESS ISN'T MINE TO GIVE OR WITHHOLD

I'm sure you've found other processes to help you work through forgiveness, but I've found some power with this one, which I was taught by a friend of mine.

First, you *reveal* you're hurt. If you want to close the door on your past and get closure so certain people don't hurt you anymore, you can do it. But there's one thing you have to remember: there is no closure without disclosure.

Second, those feelings of resentment will keep coming back, and every time they do, you've got to forgive again until you have fully *released* the offender, even if it's a hundred times or more. Writing a letter to them that you never mail will help. I've done it, and it's powerful to recognize just how much I had to say to them.

Third, is to *replace* your hurt with God's peace. When we learn to release our offenders and allow God to be in charge of settling scores, then we will discover the wonderful blessing of His peace.

Now the last part is to make *amends*. I made a list of those I've harmed and what I did. Then I thought about how I'd like someone to make amends to me. By starting this process, it helped me to refocus my life on doing God's will in my relationships.

So reach out to God and ask Him. He already knows. Don't wait until you *feel* like forgiveness, because you never will.

We all need forgiveness. I read from a book called *Love is Letting Go of Fear*, and in it, the author, Gerald Lampolsky, shares that everything we think, say, and do reacts just like a boomerang. When we send out judgements or attack others and do not forgive, they come back to us. But when we choose to forgive and refrain from making judgements and send out only love and understanding, it comes back to us.

You are a vessel for that message of love, understanding, and encouragement from the source of all peace. Utilize it.

Love is always the answer, dang it! The conclusion to my withholding forgiveness was this answer, "You probably want me to love him" so I prayed about how to do that. Then I read a story about how someone was in a similar circumstance of having a hard time forgiving someone, so I asked this of God: "but you love him, Heavenly Father. Would you give me a portion of your love for him--so I can love him too?"

5. FORGIVE YOURSELF

I know there is a level of forgiveness beyond being forgiven by others or forgiving others. The forgiveness that becomes one of the most powerful clearing methods is when you forgive yourself.

It's your perception of a situation or person that is in error. It's not the other person. Yes, they may have done something you'd prefer they hadn't done. But it's your judgement of them that causes friction. When you let go of your judgement, you free yourself. And often, when you free yourself, the other person behaves in a much more loving way. But your motivation has to come from forgiveness of yourself.

Most of us manifest a condition that can be called tunnel vision. We do not see people as a whole. We see just a fragment of a person, and our mind often interprets what we see as a fault. Most of us were brought up in a home or school environment where emphasis was placed on constructive criticism, which actually is usually a disguise for fault-finding.

6. I CHANGED THE WAY I TALK ABOUT PORNOGRAPHY ADDICTION AND IT ALL STARTS WITH MINDFULNESS

It's one thing to believe pornography is bad from a moral and religious standpoint, but quite another to understand the physiological impacts of viewing sexual images. What we've been taught about pornography and addiction was more of a story than science. It is a story filled with fear, shame, and discomfort around sexuality and media. It's the perception and shame that drives the desire to view pornography.

It's time to change the pornography story from addiction, isolation, and fear to hope, connection, and understanding.

I have learned from psychologist Cameron Staley that creating a more mindful approach to the way we talk about our sexuality and pornography includes an awareness of our emotions. Mindfulness not only helps individuals change, but it can help us as a community to understand how we talk with those who do struggle.

If you believe pornography is a problem and you want to help others, reduce the need people have for disconnecting with themselves and the people in their life by being a little more kind, a little more understanding, and nurturing connection to one another and to ourselves through mindfulness.

7. SHARING OUR STORY

At the risk of alienating friends or people in our community, or receiving criticism or even backlash for sharing this very personal story (not all people can believe that we are human and make mistakes, so judgement sometimes comes harsh in our culture), I hope that we help at least one person. I hope that by opening up, some other wife out there doesn't feel like she's terribly alone and broken, that no one in the world could ever understand the hell she's living in, suffering in silence, because she's keeping a secret from everyone around her. I know what that's like. I know that every story doesn't end as happily as ours

259

and some have had much harder challenges such as emotional or physical affairs. But this I know for sure: there is hope, happiness, and peace available to *any couple* who wants to find it.

To anyone whose heart is broken today because of infidelity or pornography use, or feels like it's never going to be better, that it's never going to end: if you need someone else's hope to lean on, you can lean on ours. Change is possible. The Savior can help you, and His atonement can heal the worst pain and the most broken hearts. The miracle of recovery is available to anyone who has a desire.

I know that we have a Heavenly Father who loves each of us more than we can possibly imagine. As Trent worked through breaking this cycle, I was mindful that there's no way a loving Heavenly Father would allow so many of His children to suffer through this without a way out.

Trent is a son of God. I believe that, and I've held on to that knowledge to get me through hard things in our past. I am so grateful we found the steps that showed us the way, and I'm so grateful for many others who've bravely shared their stories, because that ended up changing others' lives completely. And I hope that by sharing this, we can bring a few of you hope.

CHAPTER TWENTY

WHY SEX IS SO IMPORTANT IN MARRIAGE

No matter what your personal or spiritual views are on sex, I think if there's one thing that we all can agree on, it's the fact that if anyone should be gettin' it on, hot 'n heavy and on the regular, it's us married folks. Yet, as I've worked with women this past few years, they seem to have less than stellar sex lives when it comes to the quality and consistency. Why is that?

Did you know that reportedly only 48% of couples have sex on the same day that they say "I do"? They make sure that their outfits are flawless, the DJ has an unbelievable playlist and the napkins on the tables match, yet somehow, once the wedding and reception is over, sex is not a top priority.

Here's the thing about that. The word "consummate" means "to complete (an arrangement, agreement, or the like) by a pledge or the signing of a contract," "to complete (the union of a marriage) by the first marital sexual intercourse," and "to bring to a state of perfection; fulfill." This means that a marriage can be annulled if two people have not consummated their union (had sex after getting married). Did you know that back in the old-school, Jewish days, a reception didn't even get underway until the bride and groom went into a back room and had sex first? Why? Because only after sex/consummation were they considered to be "truly married."

My point? Sex is a big freakin' deal in a marriage, from the very day two people decide to become one in marriage.

So, in honor of the beauty of marriage and the powerful and extremely relevant purpose that sex serves in it, I wanted to end this book by sharing some reasons why every married person reading this should be taking full advantage of their bed and the spouse that they share it with, as often as they possibly can.

1. SEX CULTIVATES ONENESS

"Therefore shall a man leave his father and his mother, and shall cleave unto his wife: and they shall be one flesh. And they were both naked, the man and his wife, and were not ashamed."
                                        --Genesis 2:24-25

If you pay close attention to how things went down in the Garden of Eden, Adam and Eve--while it does appear that they had sex--didn't have children right away (that didn't happen until Genesis 4). They had to become one.

So yes, oneness is paramount. A word that comes to mind when I think about two people becoming one through the act of sex is fusion: "the act or process of fusing or melting together." So married folks, if you want to feel closer to your spouse, if you physically desire to "become one" with them, the transmission of oxytocin via sex is one way to make that happen.

2. SEX IS GREAT FOR YOUR HEALTH

Sex reduces stress (more on that in a bit), boosts your immune system, strengthens your pelvic floor and bladder, lowers your blood pressure, burns calories, and can help to prevent prostate cancer when it comes to your hubby too.

3. SEX IS THE ULTIMATE DE-STRESSOR

It is a proven fact that sex has a powerful way of reducing stress levels. For one thing, it releases endorphins and oxytocin so that you feel better. Sex also lowers the stress hormone cortisol in your system so that your blood pressure drops, you are less anxious, and you feel calmer. Deep breathing and climaxing also aid in making it easier to relax.

Seeing that heart disease, diabetes, headaches, depression, asthma, and obesity are all health issues that are directly connected to stress, and because stress also affects our levels of productivity, concentration, and effective communication, you can see why using sex to lower your stress levels is such a wise thing to do (especially morning sex!).

4. SEX STRENGTHENS COMMUNICATION

One of the tricks to having a simultaneous orgasm with your spouse is making sure that both of you communicate with one another. It is not at all necessary to orgasm at the same time in order to have an amazing sexual experience, but rarely would it happen without communication. What do you like? What do you want more of? What gets you there, and what is a total turn-off? How close are you and what will bring you closer to orgasm? (Some of these questions were in previous chapters, but are worth asking again and you can word them in your own way before, during or after your next sexual experience).

While it is true that not everyone enjoys "sexy talk" in the bedroom, dead silence—before or after the act—isn't great for most of us. For some couples, life is so hectic that the only time uninterrupted conversations can happen is in the bedroom. And sex? Sex is a form of intimacy, and a gateway to feeling warmth, affection, and nurturing from your spouse. So, even if there's no sexy talk during the act, be open to some pillow talk afterward in the afterglow phase.

I would argue that the primary thing that leads to divorce is poor communication. Something that can enhance communication is sex. This is a reality that definitely should not be taken lightly. The more comfortably you can talk with your spouse about sex, the more comfortably you can talk about almost anything else in your marriage.

5. SEX IS A RELATIONAL RESPONSIBILITY

This is a point that gets overlooked way too much. That said, I'd venture to say that if there is one thing that having sex does, it's that it sets us up to be very sexually self-centered. For the most part, we only think about sex as it relates to what we want and our needs. But when we make the decision to join our lives with another individual, their wants and needs become extremely important, too. Sex is no longer solely on our feel-like-it only terms; in many ways, it becomes a staple and necessity in order to keep the bond between us and our spouse healthy, solid, and strong.

Now that I'm married, it's a responsibility. It's not just about me or when I'm in the mood for it. It's about genuinely caring about the wants and needs of Trent, too.

I've read about divorce and family law and in it it states that, "a sexless marriage can sometimes be grounds of divorce based on what is known as "constructive abandonment" (I also read that a lack of sex can cause a spouse to feel not only abandoned, but also betrayed). So long as both people are physically able and there is no abuse involved (of any form), I can understand someone who has sex less than 10-15 times a year—especially year after year—would consider calling it quits. A sexless marriage is not a healthy one. In it, reciprocity is severely lacking. And in many ways, that is an irresponsible approach to marriage.

6. SEX DISCOURAGES INFEDELITY

Trent has expressed to me that there are two primary reactions and two primary factors in how a man reacts when he sees an attractive woman. The primary reactions are 1- acknowledging, "she's attractive" or 2- indulging in thoughts such as "I wonder what she's like in bed". The two primary factors as to why a man would respond one way or the other is 1- how they have trained their brain to react (putting their desire to be faithful above the natural desires of the heart of men) and 2- what their sex life is like at home.

Most infidelity stems from very little bedroom action. I'm not saying the only cause of infidelity is if you're not having sex often enough. There are of course other factors that cause someone to be unfaithful.

What I am saying is that frequent, quality sex has a big affect on your bond. When a man feels very connected emotionally and physically to his wife, there is very little temptation to look anywhere else to fill that need for connection.

7. SEX IS A SOURCE OF HEALING

Healing is such a soothing kind of word. It means "to make healthy, whole, or sound; restore to health; free from ailment" and "to free from evil; cleanse; purify."

As I was reading an article by a licensed therapist and author Dr. Sue Johnson entitled *The Three Kinds of Sex*, healing is exactly what came to mind.

Basically, what she said is "sealed-off sex" is basically about you gettin' yours, "solace sex" is sex that you have when you're looking for some type of reassurance, and "synchrony sex" is the kind of sex that provides the type of wholeness, restoration, and purification that married couples should strive for.

It's about the kind of sex that bonds you to your spouse, makes you feel safe in their presence, and provides you with a combination of both eroticism and joy. It's the type of sex that makes you feel loved, desired and completely nurtured.

Who doesn't feel better—mentally, physically and emotionally—after an experience like that? And who doesn't want to feel that way, as much as possible?

8. SEX IS A FORM OF WORSHIP

Roll your eyes if you want to, because I sure did when I first read that sex is a form of worship. But think about it. The Bible has many verses tied to sex. It has become a spiritual experience for me now on occasion when I allow God in.

Worshiping God means using His creation as He intended. This means that worship involves our mind but also that it involves our entire body.

As time moves on we tend to forget that God designed sex and it is his gift to us. Sex is to be pleasurable, shame-free and something to unify in a loving marriage.

There are studies to support that the bonding hormone oxytocin actually causes men to feel connected to a higher power whenever elevated amounts of it is in their system.

Since oxytocin is at its peak during an orgasm, sex is definitely a spiritual experience; probably one of the most powerful ones that there is.

9. SEX CONVEYS LOVE, DESIRE, AND SELFLESSNESS

An article entitled "*The Differences Between Hook-Up Sex, Marital Sex, and Making Love*" sheds some light into why sex coneys these traits. According to the author, Douglas LaB ier Ph.D., with hook-ups, it's all about using someone else's body for your own pleasure; marital sex comes from a place of emotional connection and intimacy (although conflicts and disagreements can sometimes get in the way), and making love is:

"...when you treat each other as equal human beings within your daily relationship, and you're transparent about your inner life and emotions, you automatically feel more stimulation and excitement with each other. When you feel connected as equals and yet engage each other as separate, distinct individuals as well, that generates new energy and it enhances the sexual energy between the two of you."

This is true of our attitude toward sex as well. If our attitude toward sex is all about what we get out of it instead of what we give to it, then we have the wrong perspective. Sex should be selfless, not selfish.

I think the reason why virtually all of us prefer sex in a committed relationship is that when someone stands before you and declares that they've got your back, through thick and thin, no matter what, there's a safety in that. It goes beyond desire to love and the purest form of selflessness. Commitment doesn't get any more real than when it comes to marriage.

10. SEX CAN GET YOU THROUGH IT

Another interesting read on the topic of married sex is *"How Often Married Couples Have Sex After 5,10, 20, 30 Years Together."* There is a wide range of answers, for sure. Some couples still get it on 3-4 times a week, even after many years have passed. I now believe that with all of the responsibility that comes with marriage, we married folks deserve sex!

Sometimes, it's the pure pleasure of sex that gets them through the tough times.

If sex is for anyone, it's married folks. It's pleasurable. It's fulfilling. It's also extremely necessary. For all of these reasons and more.

Wives (and husbands) reading this, from the very bottom of my heart, *GET. YOURS. OFTEN.* I can now say that with all confidence because I've seen the change in my own marriage!

But here is something else to consider. A study of 70,000 responses from 24 countries from a book called, *The Normal Bar* by Chrisanna Northrup, resulted in some interesting findings about love and sex. Couples who have a great sex life:

- Say "I love you" to their spouse every day and mean it

- Buy one another surprise romantic gifts

- Compliment their spouses often

- Have romantic vacations

- Give one another back rubs

- Kiss one another passionately for no reason at all

- Show affection publicly (hold hands, caress, kiss)

- Cuddle with one another every day

- Have a romantic date once a week that may include dressing up, dinner out, massage, and love-making

- Make sex a priority, and talk to one another about sex comfortably

- Are open to a variety of sexual activities

CHAPTER TWENTY ONE

CLOSING

Compare sex to physical exercise. If you fail to exercise, you miss the opportunity to enhance your health, and over the long-run, health declines at a faster pace than for those who do exercise. If you work out improperly, you can injure or exhaust yourself. But appropriate exercise makes you feel good and improves your health and well-being. Should you choose to, you can attain the incredible fitness of an athlete.

It's that way with sex as well. Those who go without it lose out on a source of revitalization and possibly open the door to physical and mental health disorders. For those who squander or misuse their sexual resources, sex can lead to physical and emotional pain. But for those who nourish and protect their sexuality, who use it properly with a loving and supportive spouse, sex can bring profound benefits to your body, mind, and soul.

With a healthy, connected sex life, you no doubt feel healthier, more vibrant and vigorous, with greater physical stamina and emotional strength. Your relationships with everyone, especially your spouse, are more harmonious. You feel grateful, appreciative, and more closely connected to the natural forces that give direction to your life.

> Success in relationships is like success in any other thing in life. You have to plan and prepare yourself for the trials you'll face. Because you will face them!

I love growing older with Trent, and I like to think we have aged well, too. We celebrated 18 years of marriage in 2019. No one can push my buttons like he can and make me crazy, but no one brings me more joy.

We've had our fair share of challenges, and that's okay. If you're in a rough patch right now in your marriage, it simply means you're *normal*. Everything is constantly changing. And how you feel today, you probably won't feel tomorrow.

But know this, as this is the best piece of advice I've read. I've personally been working on this in my own marriage:

> *"Men would rather feel unloved than inadequate and disrespected."*
> --*For Women Only* by Shaunti Feldhahn

The funny thing is, most of us do respect the men in our lives, but too often it turns out that our words or actions convey exactly the opposite—without our ever intending it.

Anger is often a man's response to feeling disrespected. So always assume the best, and you will find it easier to show respect.

As I've been working consciously on respecting Trent, his decisions, his goals, and his direction in growing his business, I've seen our marriage shift. As I've respected him more, I've noticed his respect and patience with me and my flaws has increased, and we feel a greater and deeper love and connection than ever before.

I heard this quote on relationships that describes very well what we've been feeling in our marriage lately:

"You must love in such a way that the person you love feels free."
--Thich Nhat Hanh

Because we love each other enough to respect each other where we are in our imperfect nature, we both feel free and connected. I feel that over the past few years, Trent has made me wings to fly. I'm better because of it. This is why I'm happiest now out of any time in our 18 years of marriage. He loves me. Every piece of my messy me.

It all started with working on me and creating more confidence in myself as a person. It started with choosing to accept an imperfect man and love him for the goodness in him. Seeing him as a son of God and respecting him in spite of his weaknesses (all of us have a weakness, but it's hard to connect with someone who only shows you part of themselves).

It started with being willing to be vulnerable enough to share our weaknesses, our doubts, our internal struggles. It started with hoping--, and then knowing--, that when we share our struggles with each other, we didn't see each other as weak, bad, or not good enough. Instead, we felt a deeper sense of connection, a desire to lift and help the one we love, and a desire to work together towards the best version of ourselves.

I take comfort in knowing that God has my back too, and more comfort in knowing that by doing it His way, I can avoid many of the issues that plague marriages today.

If you desire peace, renewal, and growth in your relationship or marriage, it may be time to reconsider your approach.

Invest in your marriage relationship the same way you would your physical fitness if you were an athlete. Give it what it needs which is time, repair, and care.

I pray that each of you experience breakthroughs in your relationships.

WHAT TO DO NEXT

Thank you so much for taking the time to read this book. It has been a pleasure sharing these ideas with you. If you are looking for what else can help you on your journey, allow me to offer a few resources and suggestions:

Send a text message for information on these additional resources.

---

*Text **RESOURCES** to (801) 505-9750 to get:

Access to Sexual Health with Sarah Facebook Group

Sarah's Suggested Bookshelf

'Sexy Time' Spotify music playlist

---

*Text **COUPLES** to (801) 505-9750 to get:

Get more information on the Couples Connection Course that Trent and I created. This is designed to take you through hard conversations as we model how we discussed difficult topics around sex, desire, discovering what our turn ons are, and how we can help the other feel loved and connected by focusing on their love language.

---

*STANDARD DATA FEES AND TEXT MESSAGING RATES MAY APPLY.

RESOURCES

Bastian, Sariah. *Beyond Breath*. Self published, 2019.

Brotherson, Laura. *And They Were Not Ashamed*. Inspire Book, 2004.

Brown, Brene. *Daring Greatly*. Avery, 2012.

Chapman, Gary. *The 5 Love Languages.* Northfield Publishing, reprinted 2015.

Chapman, Sarah. *MindStrength for Women.* Mental Work Publishing, 2015.

Corn, Laura. *101 Nights of Great Sex.* Park Avenue Publishers, 2018.

Clark, Noel. The Etiology and Phenomenology of Sexual Shame: A Grounded Theory Study. PhD dissertation. 2017.

Davis, Laura. *The Courage to Heal: A Guide to Women Survivors of Child Sexual Abuse*. New York: William Morrow, 2008.

Dee, Jay. UncoveringIntimacy.com

Dweck, Carol. *Mindset.* Ballantine Books, reprinted 2007.

Feldhahn, Shaunti. *For Women Only*. Multnomah, revised 2013.

Finlayson-Fife, Jennifer. Art of Desire Online Course.

Gottman, John, and Julie Gottman. *Eight Dates.* Workman Publishing, 2019.

Hodson, Kristin B. Instagram. @kristinbhodson

Hollis, Rachel. *Girl, Stop Apologizing.* HarperCollins Leadership, 2019.

Jampolsky, Gerald. *Love is Letting Go of Fear.* Celestial Arts. 2010.

Johnson, Sue. The Three Kinds of Sex. https://www.drsuejohnson.com/attachment-sex/three-kinds-sex/

LaBier, Douglas. The Differences Between Hook-Up Sex, Martial Sex and Making Love, https://www.psychologytoday.com/us/blog/the-new-resilience/201005/the-differences-between-hook-sex-marital-sex-and-making-love

Maltz, Wendy. *The Sexual Healing Journey: A Guide for Survivors of Sexual Abuse.* New York: William Morrow, 2012.

Mintz, Laurie. *Becoming Cliterate.* Harper Collins Publisher, 2017.

Northrup, Chrisanna, *The Normal Bar.* Harmony, 2014.

Parker, Natasha. My Official Stance on Masturbation, https://www.patheos.com/blogs/mormontherapist/2012/08/my-official-stance-on-masturbation.html

Perel, Esther. *Mating in Captivity*. Harper Paperbacks, reprint 2017.

Robbins, Mel. *The 5 Second Rule*. Mel Robbins Productions Inc., 2017.

Robinson, Marie. *The Power of Sexual Surrender*. Phocion Publishing, 2019.

Rodman, Samantha. "How to Schedule Sex, for Skeptics." *HuffPost*, https://www.huffpost.com/entry/how-to-schedule-sex-for-s_b_7104316

Wallen, Kim, and Elisabeth A Lloyd. "Female sexual arousal: genital anatomy and orgasm in intercourse." *Hormones and behavior* vol. 59,5 (2011): 780-92. doi: 10.1016/j.yhbeh.2010.12.004. Accessed July 2019.

Wheat, Ed. *Intended for Pleasure*. Revell, 2010.

FIND A QUALIFIED THERAPIST

It's possible that reading this book has made you aware that you need to seek some professional help and guidance. Although having such a realization is difficult, it's a brave and positive step. The next step is to find someone to talk to.

In my opinion, to find a good therapist it's best by word of mouth. That means you will have to have the courage to share a piece of you to someone you trust to find a therapist.

Another option is to go to the online directory for the American Association of Sexuality Educators, Counselors, and Therapists for professionals certified in sex therapy. aasect.org/referral-directory

No matter what your source, your goal is to get at least two or three names of recommended therapists.

ACKNOWLEDGEMENTS

I need to thank a man who's been very patient with me and has never given up on me. He has played every role a person can play in the writing of a book: spouse, friend, fan, critic, editor, researcher and therapist. It is no exaggeration to say this book would not be the same without him. It might not exist at all. Had Trent not chosen to love me through my disgusting bitterness, sour attitude, and complete lack of respect, we wouldn't be the sweet fruit of faithfulness, love and connection today. To me, there are not many things better than being loved by Trent. The gift he was to me on the day we wed was wonderful, but had I known the valleys we would walk through and the strength that would bloom from it, I'd never believe it was possible to have a marriage this incredible! Like everything in our life, we did it together.

Suzanne Jensen, to whom I owe my big change. She stepped up and was brave enough to tell me her story, and she was bold to call me out to analyze and be open to adjust my views about sex. She walked with me and encouraged me every step of the way. She has been the one who I talked with throughout this whole writing process. She is my biggest cheerleader and I believe she knows more than I do on this topic!

To the many friends and family members who asked, "how's the book coming along?" and offered a word of encouragement when I inevitably replied, "slowly, thank you." Every author faces a few dark moments when writing a book, and one kind word, or a comment about how you are looking forward to reading it was enough to get me to show up again the next day and keep writing.

And finally to you. Life is too short, and you have shared some of your precious time here by reading this book. Thank you.

TESTIMONIALS

"Taking Sarah's class was a great experience, and an excellent way to open better lines of communication about sex between my spouse and I. It's been such a positive benefit for our relationship - both with some new found knowledge and in helping take away some of the "taboo" feeling when it comes to discussing sexuality. Sarah genuinely wants to help married couples deepen their connection and she presents that so well in her classes. She has certainly aided in helping deepen the connection in my own marriage."

--Rachel

"I love how honest Sarah is about her experience and how that drove her passion to help other women. I found myself being more open and willing to explore with my husband. I've always been a more explorative person in the bedroom but have had to battle the control over it. I'm learning the more I love my body and understand it, the more I don't need to worry so much about control.

I'm far from perfect but listening to her share her story and being a little more educated, helped me relax more with my husband. We have more fun and feel more connected together. We are far more frequent than ever before in our 17 years of marriage. Thank you Sarah for allowing the conversation to happen and being willing to share your journey and help other women realize how normal we are and that we aren't alone."

--Brandi

"Sarah has honest intentions of educating women about having a healthy sexual understanding of their bodies and intimacy with their significant others. She is open about her own previous struggles that have led her to better understand her own sexuality, and thus driving her to share her knowledge with others.

She is attentive, honest, respectful, and truly makes you feel at ease. Her passion in this area is absolutely apparent via her actions. The best thing is that her training gets you to take a closer look at your own sexuality and opens the dialogue with your significant other to establishing a deeper sexual connection and relationship."

--Andrea

FIND SARAH HERE

Website: http://www.sarahachapman.com

Facebook: Sexual Health with Sarah

Instagram: @sarahachap

Hashtag: #sexyconfident

Made in the USA
San Bernardino, CA
31 January 2020